"Your concentration must come as easily as the breath. Fix yourself on one thing and try to hold onto it. All will come right. Meditation is sticking to one thought. That single thought keeps away other thoughts. The dissipated mind is a sign of its weakness. By constant meditation, it gains strength."

— Ramana Maharshi

MEDITATION IS NOT ABOUT EMPTYING YOUR MIND

THE ULTIMATE MEDITATION GUIDE - HOW-TO, BENEFITS, SCIENCE, TECHNIQUES, QUESTIONS & ANSWERS, AND MORE

JAGJOT SINGH

Contents

Contents

Copyright

Disclaimer

Meditation Is Not About Emptying Your Mind ("book") is intended for educational and informative purposes only and is not intended to serve as medical or professional advice.

Jagjot Singh, the author of this book is not a doctor, therapist, or medical health professional, nor does he give any medical advice. He is also not associated with any healthcare organization.

Nothing in this book should be viewed as a substitute for professional therapy or advice (including, without limitation, medical advice).

We assume that you take full responsibility for your physical and mental health. In case of severe health symptoms of anxiety, depression, or other psychological disorders, please consult a certified therapist or practitioner, and use information in this book only as a supplement to professional advice.

Acknowledgements

I would like to express my deep gratitude to great masters: Ramana Maharishi, Jiddu Krishnamurti, Shri Nisargadatta Maharaj, and Shri Ramesh S. Balsekar for their valuable teachings and insights that helped shape my mind into what it is now.

Thanks to my wife Aneesha, who showed exceptional patience and faith in my work, and my children, Rabani and Rehaan, whose presence fills me with love every moment.

CHAPTER ONE

INTRODUCTION TO THE MOST MISUNDERSTOOD PRACTICE

Have you ever had an experience where the whole world disappeared and all that was left was an indescribable silence or emptiness that pervaded your entire being? I had this experience a couple of years ago where everything in my conscious awareness disappeared.

The bliss of emptiness had such a profound effect that it changed my life forever. I left my well-paying corporate job to venture into an unknown territory. A glimpse of that emptiness or experience completely changed my perception. It mitigated all concepts, theories, ideologies, and even the spiritual quest to know oneself. The deeper I went in meditation, the more peaceful I left, and at some point, that was no "me," so as to speak of.

It was similar to the peace of deep sleep as the person with his worries, stresses, and troubles, was not there. Yet, something was there. Something that always was and always will be. I have known it. I have seen it. I am it. Can meditation make this happen for you? I don't claim that. But meditation, if you've understood the core principle, can undoubtedly slow down the mind where this revelation may happen. Irrespective of the fact whether a spiritual awakening happens or not, meditation is a helpful practice that has the potential to calm the mind. A calm mind is focused and a better decision-maker because it reduces emotional volatility.

There's a lot of buzz around meditation nowadays, but very few understand what's it all about. I would go on to say meditation has been mostly misunderstood in the western world. Even in the east, where this practice originated, people mostly follow an imported version. It is not to say that the western version is bad. There will always be benefits, no matter which meditation practice or tradition you follow.

But there's a fundamental misconception about meditation that keeps us trapped in a never-ending cycle of rumination, either in the dead past or an imaginary future, and that's precisely the problem I'm going to address in this book. There's a lot of confusion about meditation. People often say they can't do meditation or that they don't know how to do it. And that's the thing. Meditation is not something YOU do. Meditation happens. If it's not happening, then you're simply wasting time.

Confused? Don't worry. We'll get to the bottom of it. But before that, I'll introduce you to meditation both from the eastern and western perspectives. We will talk about the physical and psychological benefits, how and where to practice, why do we even need to do it in the first place, seating postures, different types of practices, breathing exercises, and in the final chapter, we'll take a look at some common questions on meditation.

We'll dive deep into what scientific studies tell us about meditation and how it affects brainwaves that significantly impact our daily living. That said, meditation is not a magical formulation or prescription to treat psychological disorders and other physical conditions. But it can be a powerful supplementary practice if you're suffering from ailments. The benefits are not why the meditation is done. Benefits happen as a consequence of mental stillness. The idea of any spiritual practice is to go deep within to inquire into the nature of the "being" that experiences the world in its own light.

Stillness comes when things are witnessed with an undistorted perception, which can happen only the mind is still. What do I mean by undistorted perception? It is where things are seen for what they are rather than what they should be. When you cultivate the ability to see things the way they are, your decisions have less bias in them. Your emotional state does not interfere in your decision-making. It is not to say that you'll never make a wrong decision in your life.

For sure you'll make wrong decisions, but you'll never carry the load of guilt for making those decisions because you'll know that you made them based on past circumstances, and that has got nothing to do with who you are at this very moment. Meditation has the potential to get rid of useless chatter of the mind. It's not that the chattering stops, but your involvement in the chatter finishes. That, in my opinion, is one of the most peaceful states of the mind.

A still mind brings out the highest creativity. It is not a thinking mind. A thinking mind is constantly engaged in incessant thinking and what-ifs. The thinking mind is more attached to the outcome of work rather than simply doing what comes naturally. A creative or working mind is an engaged mind. It doesn't care about the outcomes. It simply allows the work to happen by bringing you into a flow state where you have no sense of time.

When the thinking mind is dominant as the inner-critic or otherwise, the working mind doesn't get a chance to unleash its potential. To have a laser-like focus, the thinking mind has disappeared. Meditation is one of the practices that can help with that. Meditation allows us to access deeper states of our minds. The deeper we go, the more peaceful it becomes. At a certain point, you experience yourself as the pure unchanging awareness that is infinite and one with everything in this universe.

This mental state is the place of absolute restful calm. Reaching such depths enables us to rise above our worries, fears, anxieties, insecurities, and gives us a profound realization of the essence of the pure being that we are. When the mind is quiet, we discover who we are and why we are here. Meditation provides us a host of other benefits that I shall subsequently cover in the chapters to follow.

But an important thing to remember is that meditation is not a sprint; it's a marathon. It takes a lot of patience and consistent practice to see the actual results. But again, benefits are just the by-products of a still mind. Let's understand this through the analogy of an ocean. Our mind is like an ocean with turbulent waves at the surface, but the bottom is always quiet and peaceful. The troubled mind is the conscious mind that we use to survive in the world.

But there is a deeper layer, known as the subconscious mind. This one is extremely dominant and powerful. The habits we form by exercising our conscious mind get stored within the subconscious mind. For example, daily routine activities like brushing teeth, bathing, eating a meal, and driving down to work, are stored in your subconscious mind. You don't have to think about performing these activities. They get done automatically. While brushing your teeth, you don't have to think about where and how to move the brush. That knowledge is within the subconscious, which has come about through repeated actions.

Deeper than the subconscious mind lies the unconscious mind. The unconscious mind is the storehouse of vast amounts of information that answers deep-seated questions. Stress arises when our conscious mind is not in sync with the subconscious mind. For example, a person might claim to be very loving and spiritual on the outside but behave like a complete materialist when no one is watching.

Another example would be when people make plans and resolutions to achieve goals – these could be anything like fitness, making money, improving relationships, or merely practicing self-care. But when the time comes to take action, they don't do anything. Have you ever thought about why we fail to take action on our goals? What stops us? It is the fear that resides deep within the subconscious mind. The fear gets accumulated in the subconscious's vast depths, and some of it trickles down into the unconscious.

Meditation offers an opportunity to reach the deepest layers of mind and light up the stored afflictions. It initially feels uncomfortable, but as the stored toxic energy dissipates, it makes room for calm and tranquility. Initially, this can be an overwhelming experience, but with guidance and time, your mind will build resilience to afflicting thoughts and emotions as you witness yourself completely separated from them. Your involvement with those afflictions will finish.

Meditation reduces stress by calming the conscious mind. When the conscious mind is calm, we create space for uncomfortable stuff to come up from the deeper layers. It's important to understand that our behaviors are primarily dictated by what lies within our unconscious mind. It is extremely powerful. Unfortunately, we do not have direct access to our subconscious or the unconscious mind. And that's the reason why we become slaves to our habits and tendencies. Time and again, troubling emotions come from within our subconscious, and they can be pretty traumatic to re-experience.

When the mind makes rumination into a habit, we live continually in a state of restlessness and anxiety. Problems like stress, anxiety, and depression are just the symptoms felt in the body. The problem lies somewhere deep. We become slaves of our own minds. To free ourselves from the above ailments, we need to realize that the mind is simply an appearance in our consciousness, and it has no concrete existence of its own. Such realization itself can bring about liberation from the tyranny of the thinking mind.

It is not that we want to get rid of the mind. If we do that, we won't be able to operate in mind. All we need to do is to uncover the thinking mind. Knowing your mind, in and of itself, is freedom. Nothing else needs to be done as such. But is that even possible? I would say it is. But it requires commitment and dedication. Learning to quiet the mind is a skill, and it can only be mastered through regular practice. The ocean is deep, but it is not inaccessible.

Meditation works to synchronize the conscious with deeper layers. With enough practice, it can go even further and create a union between the conscious, unconscious, and superconscious (universal) mind. And this union is called "Yoga" in eastern spiritual traditions. But is calming the mind that easy? Well, I'd say that it's much easier to tame an untrained horse than to calm the mind. But it certainly can be achieved with discipline and consistent practice.

That said, we don't need to force ourselves into hard discipline to quiet the mind. That won't work. Meditation is simply witnessing whatever arises in the conscious mind without clinging, rejecting, or judging the content of experience. There's a lot of information on meditation and relaxation techniques to combat stress and anxiety, but what disappoints me is that majority of them (even the most reputed sites) ignore some fundamentals (which we shall cover here) when it comes to practicing meditation.

Some prerequisites are essential and should not be ignored under any circumstance; otherwise, we'll be just wasting our time. We are going to talk about a practice that just not merely brings about a temporary change in physiology to make you feel relaxed but an approach that has long-lasting effects. What I'm saying is that we should not think of meditation merely as a quick fix for stress relief. Just 15 to 20 minutes of meditation sessions can easily relax anyone. For that matter, even a 10-minute deep breathing exercise or a high-intensity workout will bring relaxation.

But these effects are temporary. Meditation practiced with the right mindset will have a long-lasting impact. Not only that, but it will also help in building emotional resilience and endurance. Meditation does something much more than induce temporary relaxation. It brings about a significant change in the way we perceive ourselves and the world. It is not about changing thoughts or blocking them.

It's about examining who is this entity that we call "me" and how it relates to the outer and inner world.

Meditation is not a new-age fad but a practice that dates back thousands of years, and many great sages and monks have practiced it throughout centuries. They didn't do it to achieve some temporary state of bliss, but to understand their mind and how it makes identifications that bring about suffering in the world.

The oldest written evidence of meditation is in the Vedas, the sacred scriptures of Hindus, dating somewhere around 1500 BCE. Over time the practice of meditation has undergone a lot of change. Many new meditation practices take into consideration the contemporary lifestyle and are most apt for modern-day living. A lot of research is going on the positive effects of meditation on treating various mental ailments.

Suffering ends with self-knowledge. In this fast-paced world of indulgences with virtual connections and 24x7 access to entertainment, we forget to spend time with ourselves. We are going to explore it all in the chapters to follow. The objective of this book is not to make you a good meditator. The objective is to end the suffering and bring about peace in daily living by understanding the nature of our own minds.

CHAPTER TWO

BENEFITS OF MEDITATION: WHAT DOES THE SCIENTIFIC RESEARCH TELL US

A word of caution before we proceed further. I don't claim that meditation all by itself has the capacity to cure life-threatening ailments. If you're suffering from severe physical and mental health issues, your first line of action should be to consult a medical health professional.

I'm not a doctor or associated with the medical field in any way, and I'm not suggesting that you use meditation as an alternative to medical treatment for severe ailments. Use meditation or mindfulness only after consulting your doctor and as a supplementary practice to your therapy or treatment.

Many people believe that meditation is "woo-woo" stuff from the east. Well, I'll take away one woo. One "woo" is fine. In this chapter, we'll take a look at meditation from a scientific perspective. Meditation is beneficial for everyone in general. Most of us feel that practicing meditation requires a rigorous routine, steel discipline, and guidance from experts. But believe me, that is not the case.

Our aim is not to become a renunciate monk and live in caves. We just want to be calmer and more relaxed, and simple meditation practice of 10 minutes a day can help us achieve that. Also, scientific studies show that meditation practice greatly contributes to our physical and mental well-being. Meditation can be practiced anywhere and at any time. It enhances your experience of the present moment (also referred to as now). It is a practice that makes us more confident and teaches us love, patience, and compassion towards ourselves and others.

It teaches us to be aware of the present moment simply, and observe our thoughts and emotions, without reacting or passing judgment on them. You start by sitting in a quiet place, in a comfortable position, preferably during the morning time (or in the evening, if that suits you), mainly because at those times you are most rested and relaxed.

Close your eyes, and be aware of your breathing sensation. Start with ten minutes every day and gradually increase the time as you start making progress. Let's explore some of the benefits of meditation.

Meditation Reduces Stress and Anxiety

We are fortunate to be living in times where there is no shortage of opportunities, yet, at the same time, it's unfortunate that stress and anxiety have become a part of life. Whether you are a student, a homemaker, or a working professional, expectations from people around you are extremely high. As a student, you have to excel academically. The conventional education system is demanding, and the pressure is from peers, parents, and teachers is always there.

If you are a working professional, the levels of stress may be higher, as you have to build worthy goals, meet deadlines, support your family, pay mortgages and loans, and manage family and relationships as well. There is no doubt that modern-day living is stressful, but like everything else, this is also manageable. It's essential to set aside a few minutes during the day to be all by yourself away from distractions and disturbances.

And whenever you sit by yourself, you'll notice that thoughts related to work, family, and home urgencies will start rushing in. That's how the mind works. It keeps us involved in thinking. The moment you begin meditation, all of sudden, thoughts of pending work and assignment, family, bills, etc., may come up. Sometimes the undercurrent of thinking is so strong that you may be tempted to stop meditation and get up. But when you're busy checking your smartphone or watching entertaining content, these thoughts won't appear. Your mind is habitually suppressing your worries by engaging in distractions such as phone, tv, books, etc. Therefore, it's natural to have worrisome thoughts when you're all by yourself. The more you suppress it, the more it leads to stress and anxiety. Your mind is continuously reacting to a chain of unproductive thoughts.

You can see through your own experience how easy it is to get involved in this chain of afflicting thoughts, one after another. These thoughts, in turn, lead to afflicting emotions that become a breeding ground for further tormenting thoughts, and the cycle continues. Suffering is getting caught up in the thinking mind. It happens to the best of people, and it is damaging to our mental and physical health.

Prefrontal Cortex or the PFC is the most evolved part of the brain, and it heavily influences the executive functions such as thoughtfulness and impulse control. This part of the brain is key to reasoning, problem solving, comprehension, and creativity, among other things. Stress is associated with decreased activity in the prefrontal cortex and is generally a cause of concern for many medical practitioners.

Dr. Sara Lazar and her team studied the effects of meditation on the brain[1]and showed increased activity in the left prefrontal cortex. They concluded that the more the subjects meditated, the better were the results. Studies show that focusing on the present moment through the regular practice of mindfulness can reduce the production of cortisol levels - the stress hormone.

It Increases Focus and Concentration

Nowadays, the ability to focus and concentrate has become difficult due to distractions like gadgets and devices, smartphone apps, social media, tablets, etc. Youngsters, especially children, get hooked to these distractions very easily. It is a known fact that our natural reserve of willpower is limited. It depletes very soon if we have to make too many decisions in a short time.

Every time we flip through news pages or social media feeds, we make several decisions about reading it or not in split seconds. This activity is very exhausting for the brain. Later on, we can't concentrate on important tasks because we have already exhausted our minds with constant decision making. This phenomenon is also known as decision fatigue.

With regular meditation practice comes clarity of mind, and our ability to concentrate on important tasks increases significantly. We begin to focus better on the task at hand rather than engage the mind in multiple unproductive tasks. Recent studies show that meditating for just 15 to 20 minutes a day can significantly improve your cognitive processing capability and IQ.

One study[2] shows that regular practice of meditation can reverse the brain pattern that contributes to poor attention span and mind wandering.

Meditation Physically Changes the Key Areas of The Brain

Meditation practice has an amazing variety of neurological benefits with enhanced connectivity between regions of the brain. Default Mode Network (DMN), or the default state network, is a large-scale brain network responsible for the wandering of the mind (also known as the monkey mind).

DMN is in the active state when our mind is clear of thoughts, and it is a well-established scientific fact that it is the monkey (overthinking) mind that is responsible for making us more worried and stressed. DMN gets activated when we think about others, remember the past, or make plans for the future.

Studies[3] indicate that regular practice of meditation decreases activity in the DMN region, making us happier and more productive. In addition to decreasing activity in the DMN region, meditation also helps preserve the brain's aging, helps reduce anxiety and depression, and leads to changes in the key areas of the brain

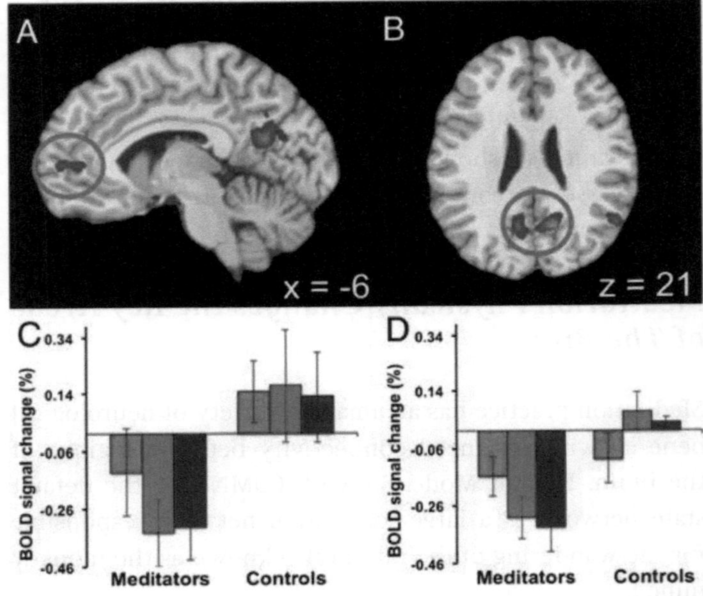

Source: https://www.pnas.org/content/pnas/108/50/20254/F1.large.jpg

The fMRI scan above shows how regular meditation practice physically changes the brain. fMRI is a safe, non-invasive instrument that measures the level of oxygen in the brain. Higher oxygen levels are associated with higher brain activity.

Helps with Addictions and Eating Disorders

Most people struggle to quit smoking, drinking, binge-watching television, and playing video games. They try hard, make resolutions year after year, only to give up after a short duration of time. These addictions and bad habits are so ingrained in our subconscious minds that it's challenging to give them up using willpower alone. I once had gained so much weight that I had to struggle for years to get to my usual weight. I became lazy, never followed an exercise regime, ate food irresponsibly and erratically, kept watching mind-numbing content on OTT platforms for hours, and did everything possible to divert my attention from thinking about my health and the ailments (like migraines and headaches) I was suffering from.

Still, nothing ever worked. My health started deteriorating, and I knew that I had to do something about it. The problem was that I was not dealing with my innermost fears and emotions. We get addictions and bad habits because we don't like to deal with the uncomfortable stuff. We feel so scared that we prefer to suppress our feelings instead of confronting them head-on. We get scared by our thoughts and divert our attention to something that gives us short bursts of pleasure. But those hidden emotions and feelings come back to haunt us over and over again.

A study[4] conducted in 2013 measured the effectiveness of Mindfulness-based intervention (MBIs)[5] for treating obesity-related eating behaviors such as emotional, binge, and external eating disorders. Traditional weight loss programs only teach calorie in vs. calorie out. Everybody knows that it's not a secret, but how many of us can implement this principle in reality? Why do we fail? And what's the solution?

Practicing mindfulness and meditation, we start understanding how our thinking patterns create afflicting emotions and addictive behaviors. Once we get to know the root of our restlessness, we become mindful of not turning to comfort foods while experiencing emotional highs.

Instead, we allow the feeling to pass and then assess what to eat and when.

Physical Health Benefits of Meditation

Meditation has become increasingly popular as more and more people discover its wide-ranging health benefits. It is a fact that meditation has many benefits on mental health, but recent studies also indicate a direct connection between meditation and physical well-being. Stress damages our body in many ways by elevating the cortisol (the body's primary stress hormone) levels. It creates havoc in the body as cortisol is responsible for regulating a wide range of processes, including the immune system and metabolism.

Elevated cortisol levels are linked with hypertension, obesity, suppressed immune system, and depression, among other abnormalities.

Some of the benefits of meditation on the physical body are as follows:

• It helps in improving the immune system[6].

• According to a 2021 study[7] published by the American Journal of Biomedical Science & Research, the heart rate decreases during meditation, and the heart rate rhythm becomes more regular as compared to before meditation.

• It helps in improving the quality of sleep[8].

• Studies[9] show improvements in people suffering from age-related memory loss. This particular meditation practice is called Kirtan or mantra chanting and is widely popular among aged people in India.

• It helps in managing pain and inflammation within the body. A large study[10] comprising of 3500 participants showed that meditation was associated with a decrease in pain.

- Recent studies[11] show that meditation can help reduce blood pressure and symptoms of irritable bowel syndrome.
- A study[12] shows that yoga-based interventions, including breathing exercises and meditation, improve Inflammatory Bowel Disease (IBD).

Meditation Produces Positive Emotions and Helps in Reducing Depression.

The practice of Loving-Kindness Meditation (LKM) helps cultivate compassion, kindness, and love for yourself and others. For you to have positive emotions for others, you should be full of positivity yourself. So, work on yourself first. You can't offer anything to anybody unless and until you don't have it yourself.

You first start by reciprocating love to people who genuinely care for you. They could be your family, friends, or relatives. With practice, you will eventually begin to radiate positivity towards all types of people. People you often see but don't know in person, like that guy or girl in the grocery shop counter, people who work in your office, or that one person who serves you food at your favorite restaurant.

And ultimately, you reach a stage where you start developing empathy and compassion, even for those who are unpleasant towards you. It could be an annoying coworker, a demanding boss, or an overbearing family member. In an analysis, which was a randomized control trial of mindfulness[13] meditation for generalized anxiety disorder, it was shown that adults who attended at least one session of MBSR showed significant improvements in anxiety.

Here's another study[14] that shows that TM (Transcendental Meditation) is more effective in treating anxiety than many alternative treatments. According to the National Institute of Mental Health (NIMH), depression is the most common mental disorder in the United States[15].

In her recent work, Gaelle Desbordes, Neuroscientist at Harvard Med School, explores the effects of meditation on the brains of clinically depressed patients. Her findings have revealed that changes in the brain activity of the subjects who had learned to meditate hold steady even when they are not in meditation.

Learning life skills should begin at an early age. These skills are essential for physical and mental well-being. But understanding these skills should be done in the proper manner, under the guidance of a compassionate teacher.

Research shows that children who meditate daily (even for just 10 minutes) have high self-esteem, high emotional quotient, higher levels of awareness (with greater attention span), and overall do well academically.

A study[16] conducted by the American Academy of Pediatrics comprising of 300 fifth to eighth-grade students shows significant improvements in depression, negative coping, rumination, self-hostility, and post-traumatic symptom recovery.

How Meditation Impacts Brain Waves

The brain is the most complex organ of the human body and has been the subject of study in the scientific community for many ages. The brain is the CPU of the entire body, and it's essential to understand what goes on inside it. Before we go deep into what brainwaves are and how to use them to our advantage, we must remember that this is a relatively new area of research.

Although neuroscientists have been studying the brain for ages, it's only recently that we have made breakthroughs and come to know about how brain activity affects our thinking and emotions. Modern science has also established that meditation significantly affects electrical activity going on within the brain.

As meditation is something you can do anytime and anyplace, you can access the part of your brain that dictates emotions. With this knowledge, you can bio-hack your way to unlimited joy and beat stress and anxiety for good. All of this can be done without you spending too much money and from the comfort of your own home.

What are Brain Waves?

Our brain is composed of billions of neurons, where each neuron connects to many other neurons in the brain. Whenever we perform cognitive activities, such as thinking, reasoning, perceiving, or decision-making, the corresponding group of neurons are lit up inside the brain, i.e., electrical signals pass back and forth between them. For example, when you drive to work, you don't have to think about the route every time because your brain is intelligent enough to light up the corresponding neurons in the brain that tells you where to go.

By repeating an action repeatedly, we train our neurons to behave in a particular manner. Our brain learns to activate the right group of neurons in different situations. When these neuron cells are active, they pass electric pulses back and forth and send messages to each other. The network of cells synchronizes their firing, and this becomes a repeating cycle known as the "brainwave."

Brainwaves, also known as neural oscillations, are how scientists measure the brain's functioning. This electrical activity within the brain is quite strong and is measured by an instrument called EEG (electroencephalogram).

In this technique, electrodes are placed on top of the scalp, where they detect the electrical pulses with the help of EEG. These electrical pulses are further visually analysed on a display monitor. This technique is known as Electroencephalography. So the next question is – how are these brain waves measured? They are calculated as the number of times the neurons are firing (cycles) electric pulses per second. These cycles (also known as frequencies) are measured in Hertz, or Hz in short.

Brain waves with lower frequencies make us feel tired and sluggish, whereas brain waves with higher frequencies correspond to more alertness and awareness.

Primarily, there are five types of brain waves:

Delta Brainwaves (0.1 – 4Hz)

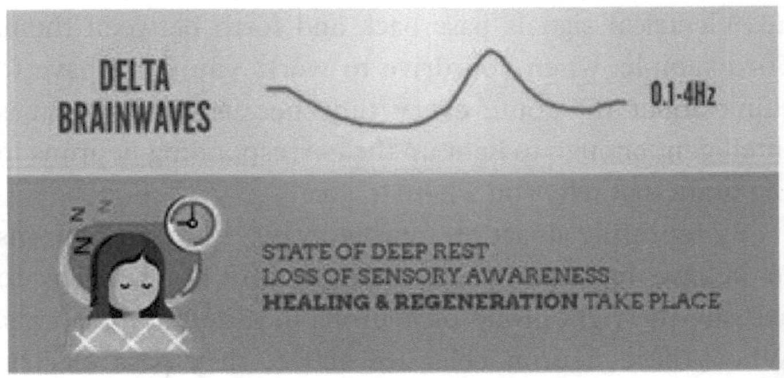

These are the brainwaves you produce when you are in a state of deep rest or sleep. Delta brainwaves are the most mysterious of all brainwaves. During the delta cycle, we are in the deepest part of our sleep, so much so, that we don't even experience any dream in this state.

It's hard to remain conscious in this state. My own take on this is that consciousness does not disappear in this state. It's just that there is nothing to be aware of because our brain changes activities in the regions that correspond to sensory inputs.

Delta brainwaves are predominant in children up to the age of 1 year (just an estimate – this is subjective). They are also the last brainwaves to be produced before we die. Zen masters and monks are said to emit delta waves during deep meditative states. In this state, there is no awareness of what is happening, but the body goes through a period of healing and regeneration.

Some experienced meditators can achieve this state of deep rest within a short time (within an hour or two), as compared to what regular people experience after a deep sleep of eight hours.

Theta Brainwaves (4 – 7Hz)

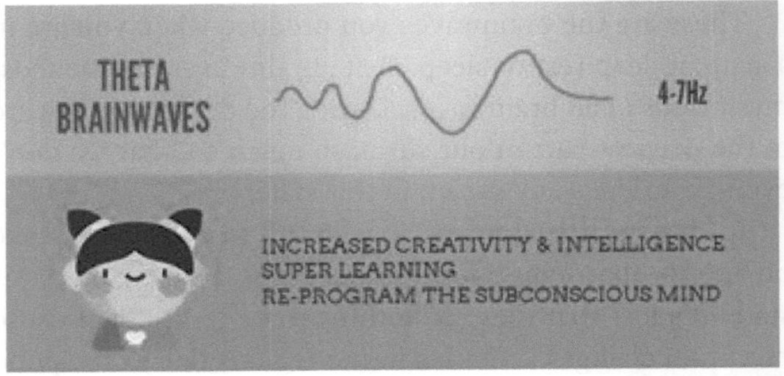

These are associated with deep meditation, and expert meditators have experienced this state, which gives deep relaxation and dream-like imageries. Theta waves are associated with daydreaming, enhanced learning, and creativity.

Time spent in theta is associated with deep physical relaxation, imagination, intuition, and emotional connection. In this state, your imagination runs wild. I'm sure you must have experienced dreams where you craft a story and are the center of attraction with remarkable capabilities. And at the same time, you experience emotions in the same way as you would when you're awake.

Kids spend a lot of time in theta. Their imagination works more than adults. That's why kids are fast learners. Theta state is associated with super-learning. They are not afraid to experiment and are open to all ideas, unlike adults who filter out information based on past experiences. There is no judgment in the theta state.

Have you ever wondered "what thinking outside the box" means? Thinking outside the box happens when your logical mind does not put constraints on your thinking. It happens when you stop judging the contents of your mind and start accepting everything. Theta brainwaves facilities this kind of thinking.

Theta waves give you the idea that "this is possible and it can happen" after that, your logical mind (in beta state) takes over and helps you to turn that thought into reality.

In fact, the theta state can help you to re-program your subconscious mind by storing information in long-term memory. The dreams experienced in heightened theta state are remembered for an extended period of time (potentially many years or even a lifetime).

Alpha Brainwaves (7 – 13Hz)

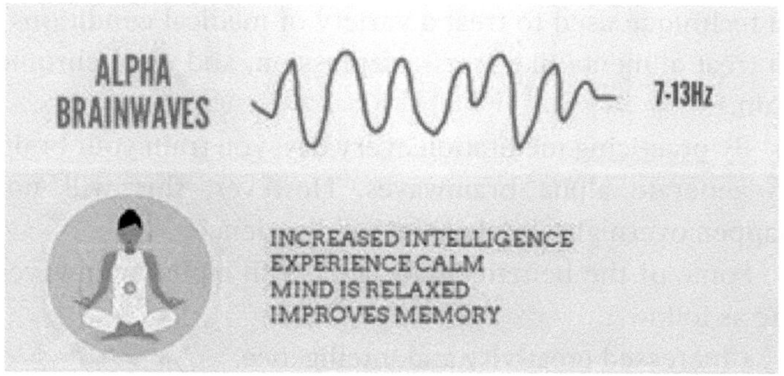

Alpha brainwaves are associated with calmness and alertness where the mind and body are in sync with each other. Alpha state is all about the 'now' or the present moment.

When you are in the beginning phase of your meditation, you transition from beta to alpha. As a result, you start experiencing more calm as the mind becomes quieter. Alpha brainwaves calm the overall nervous system and lower the heart rate.

In the alpha state, the mind is clear of unwanted thoughts, and the functioning of the senses (inputs) is minimized. This is what is experienced when we start practicing mindfulness.

Mindfulness teaches us to be in the present moment and allow the flow of thoughts in and out of mind without focusing on any one of them. With the regular practice of mindfulness and meditation, you experience the effect of alpha brainwaves.

The moment you start focusing on thoughts (either positively or negatively), you move from alpha to beta. Alpha brainwaves are linked with a relaxed state of mind; as a result, psychologists use a technique called Biofeedback (a technique used to treat a variety of medical conditions) to treat ailments like stress, depression, and even chronic pain.

By practicing meditation every day, you train your brain to generate alpha brainwaves. However, this will not happen overnight. It takes time and patience.

Some of the benefits associated with alpha brainwaves are as follows:

- Increased creativity and intelligence.
- Improved memory.
- Feeling calm and relaxed.
- High level of alertness.

One of the ways to generate alpha brainwaves is to daydream. People who are addicted to daydreaming use it as a mechanism to overcome stress and depression, which is a result of too much activity going on inside the brain. However, daydreaming is not the best way to handle this type of situation because it can become addictive and interfere with your daily life.

Beta Brainwaves (12 – 30Hz)

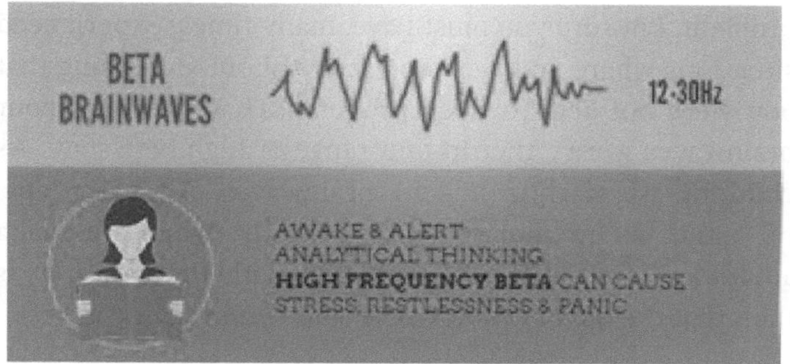

Beta brainwaves are predominant during the normal waking consciousness. Whenever we are engaged in activities like problem-solving, public speaking, or analytical thinking, beta brainwaves are at work. This is the state most people spend time in.

Beta brainwaves can be divided into three parts:

• **Low Beta (12-15Hz)** – is associated with high concentration and a focused mind.

• **Mid-Range Beta (15-20Hz)** – is associated with an increase in energy, stress, and also anxiety.

• **High Beta (20-30Hz)** – is associated with high stress, anxiety, restlessness, paranoia, and depression.

In this state, your mind is sharp and completely focused. If you are working on solving a complex problem that requires unwavering attention, this is the state you want. In beta, the neural activity is at its maximum.

However, too much beta activity in the wrong parts of the brain is associated with chronic stress, anxiety, and even depression. On the other hand, insufficient beta activity is associated with ADHD[17].

Sometimes even too much excitement becomes a problem. I'm sure you must have, many times, experienced situations where you were so excited about something that you were not able to sleep properly. That's because your brainwaves were either in mid-range or high beta state. As children, we start with delta brainwaves. After a couple of years, we go into theta, and finally, when we reach adulthood, we start full interaction with the world. It is then that the beta brainwaves become dominant.

Gamma Brainwaves (32 – 100Hz)

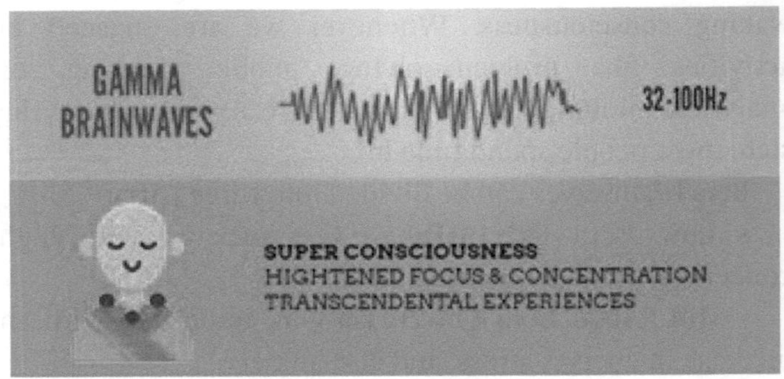

These are extremely fast oscillating brainwaves with the smallest amplitude and are associated with 'super consciousness' and peak performance. Gamma waves indicate a high level of cognitive functions, and they are easily seen in experienced meditators.

These brainwaves were unknown for a long time because the analog EEG could not detect brainwaves higher than 20Hz. With the advent of digital EEGs, gamma brainwaves were discovered.

People with high gamma brainwaves show the following characteristics:

- High IQ.
- Increased intelligence.
- Increased memory recall.
- Increased sensory perception.
- High degree of focus and concentration.
- High degree of self-control.
- High compassion.
- Increased happiness and feelings of joy.

In the case of gamma, it is observed that neurons in different regions of the brain fire in harmony. A natural way to generate gamma brainwaves is to meditate. Meditation especially on love and compassion can help in generating gamma brainwaves.

Gamma brainwaves have been extensively studied on Buddhist monks (using fMRI imagery), and it was found that the monks were able to achieve this state in a short burst of time, and this was demonstrated with visuals on the display monitors.

Not only that, but the monks were able to enter and leave these states at will. This indicated their laser-like focus and ability to generate compassion at will and with ease. Even when they were not meditating, their brainwaves exhibited characteristics of gamma waves. All of us generate gamma brainwaves, but for regular people, this lasts only for a fraction of a second, whereas, in the case of experienced meditators, it goes on for almost a full minute.

Also, the low production of gamma brainwaves is linked to lower mental processing, poor memory, and learning difficulties. A research study[18] suggests that meditation may boost gamma wave production. However, in my opinion, producing gamma brainwaves is no easy feat. It requires years of meditation practice to even achieve theta levels which are mostly seen in Himalayan monks.

Hack Your Brain to Beat Stress and Anxiety

Modern-day lifestyle is hectic, chaotic, full of uncertainty, and high expectations. It's an unfortunate reality that most people have accepted stress and anxiety as something normal. This is not a very healthy way of living. If you are suffering from anxiety, you should accept the fact that it's unhealthy, that you deserve to live an anxiety-free life, and that you have to do something about it.

From the above discussion, it is evident that anyone suffering from anxiety and depression is spending most of their time in a high beta state. So the idea is to hack our brain and transition from high beta to either low beta or theta. So how do we do it?

One way is to take prescription medications or recreational drugs. However, great caution must be exercised if you're going down this route. And this must be done in consultation and under the supervision of a certified medical practitioner. Also, do consider the possibility of some gut-wrenching and life-threatening side effects. Another way is to practice mindfulness and meditation. We have lots of resources on this blog to get you started with meditation and mindfulness. However, don't expect an immediate result. You have to train your mind sufficiently before you see any substantial result.

The idea is to form a daily meditation (10 – 20 minutes is good enough for beginners) routine and stick to it. Eventually, you will start noticing a great deal of change in your mood as your brainwaves transition from high frequency to lower frequencies. Even a change from high beta to low beta will completely transform your life.

Some of the expert meditators who have been practicing meditation for years easily transition from lower beta to alpha and theta states. In these states, their mind slows down giving a very calming feeling. You must have often heard the phrase slow down. What that basically means is that you slow down your mind by taking it easy. When you constantly operate under stress you generate high-frequency beta brainwaves, and that in turn generates anxiety within you.

With the regular practice of meditation, you will learn to "slow down" your mind. When you perform each action with full consciousness, there's no way any amount of stress or anxiety can creep inside of you. Slowly with time, you will start noticing how your mind is becoming calm and relaxed. We have lots of resources on this blog to help you get started with mindfulness and meditation. There's no need to go to a 'guru' or expensive retreats.

Meditation can be practiced in many ways (body scan, walking, loving-kindness, mantra), and there's absolutely no dogma attached to it. You can start practicing meditation from the comfort of your home. Dalia Lama has been actively involved in studying the effect of meditation on the brain and has been encouraging Tibetan Buddhist monks to participate in such studies. It has been scientifically proven that meditation leads to an increase in the gray matter in the frontal area of the brain[19].

What Else?

Much research is being conducted on meditation, and we've just begun to scratch the surface of this fantastic ancient practice. It is our ignorance that we believe ourselves to be more advanced than ancient cultures.

The ancient people, including the yogis and sages, knew a science that we're just beginning to understand. We call ourselves advanced, and even with all the scientific and technological advancements, we still don't know the cause and cure for significant lifestyle diseases. But unfortunately, the mainstream media, including the news, do not highlight and acknowledge the people who are working relentlessly for human betterment.

Just as we do daily activities such as brushing, sleeping, exercising, socializing, etc., we can also take some time to incorporate meditation into our daily routine. Human beings are a combination of mind-body complex, and just taking care of only the physical body is not enough. Prioritizing mental health is the need of the hour and should not be ignored. Only then will we be able to tap into its infinite potential.

Now that we are convinced about the benefits of meditation and its science, let's learn to do the actual thing. In the following chapter, we learn how to meditate and build a daily routine.

[1] https://www.washingtonpost.com/news/inspired-life/wp/2015/05/26/harvard-neuroscientist-meditation-not-only-reduces-stress-it-literally-changes-your-brain/?noredirect=on&utm_term=.72f37f85b07d

[2] https://pubmed.ncbi.nlm.nih.gov/23643368/

[3] https://www.ncbi.nlm.nih.gov/pmc/articles/PMC5866730/

[4] https://www.ncbi.nlm.nih.gov/pmc/articles/PMC4046117/

[5] https://www.ncbi.nlm.nih.gov/pmc/articles/PMC5870875/

[6] https://www.pnas.org/doi/10.1073/pnas.2110455118

[7] https://biomedgrid.com/pdf/AJBSR.MS.ID.001736.pdf

[8] https://academic.oup.com/sleep/article/37/9/1553/2416992

[9] https://pubmed.ncbi.nlm.nih.gov/26445019/

[10] https://www.ncbi.nlm.nih.gov/pmc/articles/PMC5368208/

[11] https://www.nccih.nih.gov/health/meditation-in-depth

[12] https://pubmed.ncbi.nlm.nih.gov/26667293/

[13] https://www.ncbi.nlm.nih.gov/pmc/articles/PMC3772979/

[14] https://pubmed.ncbi.nlm.nih.gov/24107199/

[15] https://www.nimh.nih.gov/health/statistics/major-depression.shtml

[16] https://publications.aap.org/pediatrics/article-abstract/137/1/e20152532/52797/School-Based-Mindfulness-Instruction-An-RCT

[17] https://www.ncbi.nlm.nih.gov/pmc/articles/PMC4973024/

[18] https://www.ncbi.nlm.nih.gov/pmc/articles/PMC5261734/

[19] https://news.harvard.edu/gazette/story/2011/01/eight-weeks-to-a-better-brain/

CHAPTER THREE

HOW TO MEDITATE? AND BUILD A DAILY HABIT

I assume that most of you are beginners, so I'll keep it simple and suggest a practice that is of short duration. But before we do that, let me explain the seating posture for meditation. Now, a comfortable seating posture is crucial because meditation requires us to sit still for some time, somewhere between 10 minutes to 1 hour.

Sitting in the wrong posture will not only hinder your meditation session but can also cause serious injury to body parts. Having gone through some severe injuries during the early periods of my meditation practice, I highly suggest that you take full precaution. Traditionally, four postures (actually there are more, but let's stick to four for now) are recommended.

These are as follows:

The Easy Pose (Sukhasana)

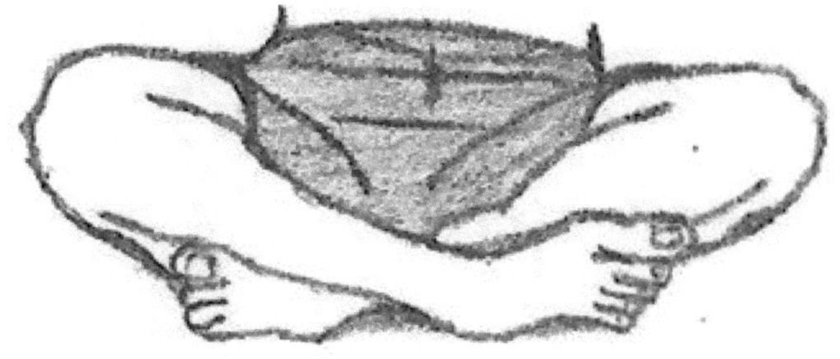

As the name suggests, this is an easy way to sit in meditation. Cross-legged posture is most recommended if you're a beginner. To make your sitting more comfortable, you can use a meditation cushion known as the zafu. The zafu elevates your hips above your knees, thereby reducing pressure on them, and it also prevents the legs from falling asleep.

The Lotus Pose (Padmasana)

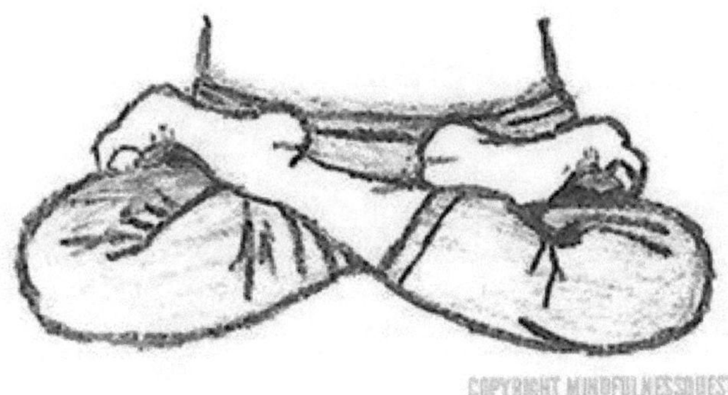

In this pose, the left leg rest above the right thigh and the right one above the left thigh. Traditionally, this is considered to be the best posture for meditation.

However, this pose is for advanced yoga practitioners who have lots of flexibility in their hips and knees. I would not recommend this pose to beginners. If you want to master this posture, you must work on building flexibility in the middle and lower parts of your body.

The Half Lotus Pose

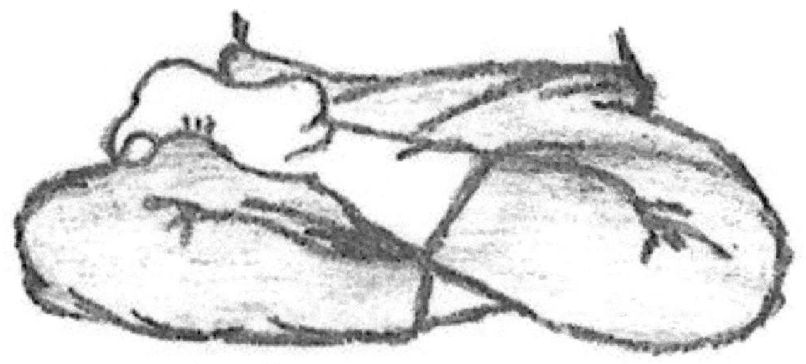

The half lotus pose is slightly easier than the full lotus because only one of the legs rests above the thigh. But still, I would not recommend this to an absolute beginner. Sitting in the lotus postures requires developing great flexibility.

The Kneeling Pose (Vajrasana)

The kneeling pose, also known as the thunderbolt pose, is most suitable for people who have stiff thighs. This is one of my personal favorites as it takes the pressure off the back. The image above shows how to sit in the kneeling pose.

Just make sure that your heels are wide apart – supporting your buttocks, and the toes slightly touching each other. If you feel too much pressure on the legs – use a seiza meditation bench for support.

What To Do If I Can't Sit for Meditation?

What about those who can't sit in the above-mentioned postures? Don't despair. This is very common. Although

I have been practicing meditation for over six years now, even I can't sit in some of the above-mentioned postures for too long.

If you're an absolute beginner and you feel that your legs and back hurt while sitting in the above-mentioned postures, please feel free to meditate sitting on a comfortable chair. You will not be less of a meditator if you take the help of a chair for your meditation.

You can also take the help of a meditation bench or a meditation cushion if you desire. These products are specially designed for meditation, and they offer a much more pleasant experience as compared to a regular chair or pillow. Whichever posture you choose, please ensure that you don't force yourself to sit in discomfort. Sitting in discomfort will divert your attention towards the discomfort, and that will prevent you from experiencing the relaxation you desire.

Steps to Practice Meditation

Meditation is something you can easily practice from the comfort of your home. We'll start with an easy to follow 10 minutes breathing meditation practice.

1. Find a quiet place in your house where no one is likely to disturb you for the next 10 minutes or so.

2. Put your phone on DnD (Do Not Disturb) or silent.

3. Sit in a comfortable posture of your choice. Make sure that you are absolutely comfortable. If you find it hard to sit in the traditional yoga poses, just sit on a chair. Put cushioning where ever it's required. Whatever you do, just make sure that your spine is straight.

4. Now close your eyes and bring your awareness to this present moment. Stay in this moment for a minute or two.

5. After that take note of any sensation arising within your body. Be still and simply observe these sensations for another minute or two. Don't open your eyes to look at the clock. Just imagine the time passing.

6. Now bring your awareness to your breathing. Observe the movement of breath as it enters and leaves your body. Continue this process for the rest of the duration.

7. It is very likely that your mind will be bombarded with random thoughts at this point. But that's okay. It is expected. Don't try to forcefully block your thoughts. Whenever you find yourself distracted, just bring back your awareness to breathing again.

8. Don't try to judge your meditation session while you're doing it. The mind will play all kinds of tricks to divert your attention. Don't give into it.

9. After 10 minutes or so, open your eyes, rub your hands, and just wait for a minute or two before you get up. Don't get up abruptly. Do it slowly and gently.

And that's it. This is a simple meditation that is extremely easy for anyone to get started. The only important thing is consistency. In the next section, we will discuss how to form a daily meditation routine.

How to Form a Daily Meditation Habit?

Here are a few pointers that will help you make the most out of meditation sessions and form a daily meditation routine that you can effortlessly stick to.

Pick a time and place where no one disturbs you

When you are just starting meditation, it's better to choose a place inside your house where no one is likely to disturb you for the next couple of minutes. It can be any place like your room or the living area. You can also inform other people in your house not to disturb you for 10 to 15 minutes. Although meditation can be practiced anytime, I find early morning time to be the best because everybody is fast asleep, and there's practically no disturbance.

There is no hard and fast rule if you prefer evening time, or afternoon, it's totally up to you. But the main point is that you should have your space with no disturbances. Since you are new to this practice, it's natural that your mind will have trouble focusing and will often wander away in thoughts. So, ideally, you want to be in a place of minimum disturbance.

At times you will feel that you have just wasted your time sitting with closed eyes. You may even fall asleep while meditating. Again, it's normal. I used to feel the same when I started. But you're not wasting time. You are training your mind to focus and teaching your body to relax, so be patient. If there are noises and disturbances around, it will be difficult for you to focus, so choose a time and place where nobody disturbs you for the next couple of minutes. I have been practicing meditation for the past seven years. And now I have trained my mind in such a manner that I can meditate standing even in the middle of a crowded subway station. But in the beginning, you should be kind and gentle to your mind and body. Don't expect to just learn and behave in a particular manner in a short period.

Eliminate all sources of distraction

Elimination or minimizing distractions is perhaps one of the most crucial steps in starting meditation. It is better to ensure that you have no distractions around while you are meditating. Turn off your television, smartphones, and other devices that send out periodic notifications. I generally keep my phone and all other electronic devices off and distant from myself before starting meditation.

The reason is that while meditating, we usually get thoughts like "Oh that urgent email I was supposed to get from the client," "I wonder how many likes did I get on the picture I posted on Instagram yesterday," "did I leave the house door open," "I have to complete my project report. Why am I wasting time?" "I should workout rather than sit here," and so on. If your phone is nearby, you will be tempted to break your meditation to check your phone, and the whole exercise will be fruitless. If you can't switch off your phone (like setting up a timer for your meditation), put it on Do Not Disturb (airplane) mode.

Allow nature to help you

Open the doors and windows of your room. Let the light and fresh airflow. Nature is very kind to us and provides us with all of the elements that help nourish our minds and bodies. Natural light has a calming effect on our minds compared to the artificial lighting in the room. Feel the natural sunlight on your body and inhale fresh air for a couple of minutes before starting your meditation session. In case you have a house where you don't get enough light or fresh air, go out for a couple of minutes, do a little deep breathing and then come back for meditation.

Choose a comfortable seating posture

Posture is fundamental in meditation. It's essential to choose a position that feels comfortable and allows you to fully relax during meditation. Selecting an uncomfortable seating posture will create discomfort in various parts of your body and distract your mind by bringing attention to the pain. If you are new to the practice, you can either sit on the ground in a cross-legged position or sit on the chair with the back straight.

Most of us see those Instagram pictures of experts sitting in complicated yoga postures, and we feel that that is the only way to practice meditation. But it is not so. I know people who have been meditating for many years and can sit still on a chair for a couple of hours in a row.

Bring your awareness to the breath

Sit comfortably, close your eyes, and bring your awareness to the gentle movement of breath in and out. Don't try to force your breath; maintain the natural rhythm, being mindful of any feelings or thoughts that arise. If you find your mind wandering away in your thoughts, gently bring back your awareness to your breath. Don't feel bad if your mind gives you a hard time. This wandering used to happen a lot to me, especially in the beginning phases.

Achieving a still mind is a skill that takes time and patience. As a society, we have become so used to instant gratification that we resent doing any work where the progression is slow. At times, you will feel that you can't focus on the breath for the entire duration of your meditation session. But don't be hard on yourself. These things happen in the early stages. What's important is that you stay consistent and practice every day.

Commit to a short period of time - especially in the beginning

When you are starting, commit only for 10 minutes or less in a day. It is tempting to meditate for long when you start seeing the results, but I suggest you keep your duration short in the early stages. Because at this stage, we are just trying to form a habit. We don't want to overdo and burden ourselves. Remember, if you have decided to make meditation a part of your life, it's going to be a long journey, so prepare yourself accordingly.

Ten minutes a day is sufficient to get started. Form a routine first, stick to it for some time, and gradually increase your session time as you progress. If you find ten minutes long, do it for five minutes or even two minutes. Get started! But don't force yourself to sit for a long time.

After finishing your meditation, slowly open your eyes, bring your awareness back to the world, and gently get up and get going with other work. Don't immediately pick up your smartphone or switch on the television. Remain in that space of serenity and tranquility for a couple of minutes. Give it a few minutes because the body takes some time to adapt to the transition from the inner world to the external world.

Avoid Eating the Wrong Foods

Diet plays a major role and has a great influence on our meditation sessions. Make sure that you are on an empty stomach for the past 2 to 3 hours before you start meditation. For example, if you had lunch at 1:00 PM, wait for at least 4:00 PM to begin your session. You must understand that when you consume a meal, all the organs in your body start working to digest that food.

This process takes at least 2 to 3 hours, and if during that time, you sit for meditation, you will feel uncomfortable. It will be hard to bring focus. You will feel sleepy and lethargic and most probably will drift off to sleep. So, it's important that we need to be on an empty stomach to practice meditation, but we should also not be starving. If you're hungry for an extended time, you might not be able to concentrate because all your attention will be on thinking about food.

However, there's an exception here. It is okay to practice meditation when you get up in the morning in a fasted state. At the time, the body is relaxed, and we don't need to eat anything immediately.

I Fall Asleep While Sitting in Meditation. What To Do?

Feeling sleepy while meditating can happen when either your daily night time sleep has been insufficient or when you've consumed a heavy meal. Also, when an overactive mind is told to focus on one object such as the breath, it revolts and tries all kinds of tricks to divert attention from the object of meditation. Inducing sleep to break meditation is one such ploy of the mind.

If you practice the traditional meditation like the one I explained in the previous sections, it's likely that you'll fall asleep in the initial stages, but with continued practice, you will be able to overcome this issue. Please note that you shouldn't force your mind to concentrate. It's okay to break the meditation when the mind is too sleepy. Forcing the mind is not a good idea. Let it get used to the routine slow and steady.

For those who feel sitting in meditation is not for them, what if I tell you that there's another style of meditation that you can practice in lying down position, and it's equally effective as the traditional one. It's called the Yogic Sleep Meditation or *Yoga Nidra*, which I'll explain in the coming chapter.

Discomfort And Pain Experienced in Meditation

Body and mind are intricately connected. Just as a physical injury perturbs the mind, an anxious mind adversely affects the body. Human beings are psychophysical creatures – a mind-body complex acting in tandem. When we suppress some affliction, its effects manifest in the physical body as pain and discomfort. Some of these are mild, and we don't feel them so often daily.

However, in meditation, we frequently experience these sensations. As the mind settles down, we become sensitive to even the slightest intensity. Please note that I'm not speaking about the pain and discomfort we experience due to injury or tightness in body parts such as knees, hips, lower back, or neck.

I'm referring to the minor discomforts like itching or painful stinging sensations we commonly experience while meditating. There's not much significance to these minor discomforts. They're just a form of release in the body. At times, they may feel intense but are generally harmless. So, what do we do about them?

Don't Fight with The Uncomfortable Sensations

Generally, we carry a negative attitude towards uncomfortable sensations, and we want to get rid of them at any cost. But this attitude, in and of itself, becomes a hindrance to the meditation practice.

Being more accepting of the pain or other bodily discomforts (in bearable limits) will eventually reduce their frequency of occurrence. When you don't fight or offer resistance, they go away by themselves after playing around for a couple of minutes. A particular body part that feels tense needs to expend the accumulated energy. This idea forms the basis of practicing yoga postures where we stretch different body parts to release energy tensing up in the localized regions.

When sitting for long periods in meditation, it is common to feel the tension in lower body parts such as the lower back, hips, and knees. Whenever you experience discomfort in any body part, observe the sensation without labeling it. As you do that, gently breathe into that area of sensation. Over time, you'll notice a decrease in the intensity of the discomfort. The idea is to let go of the pain and discomfort by acknowledging and accepting it. Every time you do it, you release some of the accumulated energy in the concerned body parts.

Please remember that you should be extremely gentle with your body while performing this practice of observing the pain with love and kindness. If the discomfort is too much, break the posture by all means. Don't force yourself to sit in pain if you can't bear it. Let me elaborate a little more on this with a practical example. When we experience a headache, our initial thought is to get rid of it as soon as possible. The easiest option at that moment is to pop a pill and make it go away.

However, this kind of suppression never helps in the long run. The headache reappears with higher frequency and greater intensity. After a certain amount of time, the brain becomes tolerant of the medicine, and it stops working. Energy accumulation can happen for many reasons. One I can think of is poor posture. The modern lifestyle demands are such that we spend long hours working sitting on a chair. It makes the back muscles weak.

When we meditate sitting in complex postures such as cross-legged, the weaker muscles cannot support the lower body structure, and hence, we experience soreness and pain. Additionally, there can be psychological reasons for pain as well. For example, reoccurring headaches may happen as a result of high stress. Pain is an indication from the body that something needs correction. In addition to physical exercises, mindful living, and other corrective actions, paying attention to the pain while meditating can help hasten the process of energy release in the particular body part. Headache is merely an effect or symptom of energy imbalance and not the primary cause.

That said, if the pain is unbearable, it can be a severe issue that needs medical or professional intervention. In such cases, don't rely on meditation alone for the cure. When I talk about "observe the pain and discomfort in meditation," I assume that you can discern destructive pain - the one that needs medical treatment, from the mild pain that comes about because of the muscle tension.

There are specific pains that require expert treatment, and we should never ignore them. Some of them are as follows:

- Any kind of shooting pain should not be managed on your own by observation.
- Any continuous pain (dull or sharp) that doesn't go away on its own and poses challenges in day-to-day functioning.

In such cases, use meditation as a supplementary practice in addition to medical treatment. I have personally seen some people acting very stubborn when it comes to yoga and meditation. Despite shooting pain, they remain unwilling to compromise on their seating posture. Such an attitude is dangerous and can lead to permanent damage to the body.

What Else Can We Do to Reduce Pain?

As I mentioned earlier, most of us spend a lot of time sitting on chairs. As a result, we develop flexibility issues in the different parts of the body, especially the lower ones like the lower back, hips, hamstring, and knees.

One common problem people face while meditating is that one or both legs become numb sitting in a cross-legged position. For example, tightness in the hip area may stop the blood flow to the legs, and as a result, the leg goes to sleep.

The following yoga poses are helpful in opening up the hips:

- Bound Angle Pose (Baddha Konasana)
- Child's Pose (Balasana)
- Cow Face Pose (Gomukhasana)
- Easy Pose (Sukhasana)

Daily practicing the above yoga poses will help develop flexibility in your hips to sit in a cross-legged position. Also, you can buy a Zafu. Zafu is a comfortable meditation cushion specially designed for meditation.

It eases the pressure on the legs by raising the hips.

If you are a beginner, don't attempt to sit for a very long time in meditation. Avoid complicated postures like lotus or half lotus. What matters is not the length of time but the comfort you experience in meditation.

As beginners, our focus should be to form a daily routine, so just 10 – 15 minutes every day is good enough to get started. All of the discomforts, like aches, itches, and minor pains, result from suppressions and repressions that get accumulated as energy and create stagnation in different body parts.

Don't pay too much attention to these as they will resolve on their own with time. Don't torture yourself to sit in uncomfortable poses. *The idea of meditation is not to become a better meditator.*

At times, meditation may not leave you with a pleasant experience, and that's okay. We have to accept the afflictions which arise from within without resistance or judgment, to let go of them. It is a slow process, so give it time.

Breathing Exercises for Stress Relief

For people who find it difficult to sit in meditation with their eyes closed, breathing exercises are a great way to let go of the build-up stress. These exercises are not a replacement for meditation, but they are extremely effective for people suffering from stress and anxiety. However, as a caution, do consult your healthcare practitioner before including them in your daily routine.

It's better to practice *pranayama* or breathing exercises before starting meditation. These exercises help in increasing the flow of the *prana*, or life-force energy within the body. They promote vitality and relieve the mind from stress.

It's not mandatory to practice these exercises along with meditation in one go. For example, if you like to meditate in the evening, you can practice breathing exercises in the morning or even in the afternoon. I, however, like to do it one go. But that's just me.

Practicing these techniques for about 10 to 15 minutes before meditation will sufficiently relax your body, and help you to build better focus during your meditation session. It's imoprtant to practice these techniques on an empty stomach.

Bellows Breathing Exercise

Bellows breathing (aka *Bhastrika* Pranayama) is a traditional breathing exercise that increases the flow of prana (the life-force energy) within the body. This breathing exercise involves forced inhalations and exhalations that result in a sufficient supply of oxygen to the brain. Bhastrika invokes the fire element that is responsible for regulating thirst, hunger, energy, and metabolism of the body.

Practice Duration: 2 - 3 mins

Caution: You should be on an empty stomach for at least 2 hours. It should not be practiced by pregnant women. The elderly and people with health complications should do it slowly.

How to practice:

• Sit either in Vajrasana (kneeling or thunderbolt pose) or Sukhasana (cross-legged pose)

• Close your eyes and start deep inhalations and exhalations. Expand your lungs and your diaphragm to the maximum capacity. But don't apply too much force.

• Make sure that you maintain a steady pace.

• Take breaks in between by switching back to normal breathing.

Benefits:

• It rejuvenates the mind by removing fatigue and lethargy.

• Increases the lung capacity and rids them of the phlegm.

• Strengthens immunity.

• Energizes the body and mind.

• Helps in relaxation and promotes sound sleep.

• Helps in respiratory ailments such as cold, flu, sinus, and bronchitis.

• Helps in reducing inflammation in the body.

• Very helpful in headaches and migraines.

• Provides benefits to the entire nervous system.

• Improves focus and concentration.

Alternate Nostril Breathing Exercise

Alternate nostril breathing, also known as the *Nadi Shodhana* pranayama, is one of the most well-known breathing exercises that reduce stress, anxiety, and rejuvenate the mind. The word 'Nadi' refers to the subtle energy channels through which the 'prana' or the life-force energy flows, and 'Shodhana' means clearing of impurities.

In other words, this breathing exercise clears the spiritual energy channels by allowing the life-force energy to flow within.

Practice Duration: 2 - 3 mins

Caution: You should be empty stomach for at least 2 hours. People with health complications should do it very slowly.

How to Practice:

- Sit in any comfortable posture of your choice.
- Now close your right nostril with the right-hand thumb and inhale through the left nostril.
- Inhale slow and deep and hold for 2 seconds.
- Let go of the thumb (right hand), close your left nostril with the index and the ring finger combined, and exhale through the right nostril.
- Wait for 2 seconds after full exhalation.
- Keep your left nostril closed with the index and the ring finger, and inhale deeply through the right nostril.
- Wait for 2 seconds, release the left nostril and simultaneously close the right nostril with the right thumb, and exhale through the left nostril.
- This completes 1 full breathing cycle.
- Repeat the full cycle 5 to 10 times.

Benefits:

- Calms the nervous system and induces a state of complete relaxation.
- Improves digestion and sleep disorders.
- Removes toxins from the body.
- Oxygenates the lungs and improves breathing capacity.
- Lowers the heart rate.
- Makes you more aware.

Make sure that your rate of breath inflow matches the outflow. Also, don't use excessive force while practicing this exercise. People who have problems like heart disease and high blood pressure should perform this exercise very slowly.

Breath of Fire Breathing

Kapalabhati Pranayama is a yogic breathing technique that is performed by exhaling from the mouth in short bursts. Kapalabhati literally means "skull shining" or "brain cleansing." It is also called "Breath of Fire" because it resembles the quick, fiery exhalations of fire. It resembles a bellows in action. Kapalabhati Pranayama helps to purify the blood, improve digestion, and increase the gastric fire.

Kapalabhati pranayama is a breathing technique that is done by the practice of forcefully exhaling air from the lungs. It stimulates the nervous system and helps remove toxins from the body.

Some of the benefits of breath of fire include:

- Improves digestion.
- Relieves stress.
- Enhances concentration.
- Increases oxygen to the brain (source).

There are three steps to performing kapalabhati pranayama:

1. First, inhale deeply through your nose for 4 seconds.
2. Next, exhale quickly and forcefully through your mouth for 8 seconds.
3. Finally, inhale deeply again for 4 seconds before repeating the cycle of 8 seconds of forceful exhalation followed by another deep inhalation.

Caution: Pregnant women or people who have heart-related ailments should avoid this exercise or do it under expert supervision. You should empty on stomach for at least 4 hours before you do this exercise.

Some Important Precautions (Please Do Not Skip This)

All of these exercises are generally safe, but people suffering from various health complications should exercise caution while performing them. In such cases, it is best to consult a medical practitioner or general physician.

Here are some of the precautions:

• Women undergoing pregnancy should completely avoid all of the above breathing exercises.

• Aged people should practice these exercises very slowly.

• People with high blood pressure or heart disease should perform these exercises very slowly. No force should be applied at all. It's better to do these exercises under the supervision of an expert teacher.

• You should be on an empty stomach when you practice these exercises. Never do them immediately after a meal.

• Take short breaks in between.

• Don't eat or drink anything in between (not even water). If by mistake you drank water or tea, wait for at least 10 to 15 minutes before you resume the exercises.

My personal experience is that these breathing exercises alone are very effective in sufficiently reducing stress and anxiety. Not only that, but they also provide a host of other physical and mental health benefits. According to ancient scriptures, these breathing exercises are considered to be a type of meditation within themselves.

Keep at It

Whatever meditation schedule you choose for yourself: whether it's once a week, twice, thrice, or daily, make sure to stick to it. But also, don't feel bad if that doesn't happen in the early stages. It takes a while to build a routine. The progression of any habit is non-linear initially.

CHAPTER FOUR

AN OVERVIEW OF DIFFERENT TYPES OF MEDITATION PRACTICES

There are hundreds of meditation techniques and it's not possible to cover each and every one of them in a single article, so I have decided to cover only a handful of the most widely known and easy follow practices.

Mindfulness Meditation (Samatha)

Mindfulness meditation or samatha is a widespread Buddhist practice that helps develop calmness and clarity of mind. For beginners, this is usually the starting point of meditation. Samatha is a meditation technique that involves maintaining awareness of the breath, observing the flow of air, in and out of the nostrils. This is something easy to practice across all age groups.

If you have never meditated before, practicing Samatha meditation can be a good starting point. The objective here is to allow the flow of feelings and emotions through our minds without invoking any kind of reaction to them. Many people have a misconception that we need to completely stop the flow of thoughts in their minds. As a result, they try to do it forcefully and when they're unable to do so, they get disheartened.

Our body has been designed in such a manner that it's impossible to stop thoughts altogether. But yes, we can reduce the frequency of these thoughts and more importantly be indifferent to the afflicting ones. Trying to fight with your mind is futile. With regular meditation practice, you become more resilient to the afflicting thoughts and emotions arising in your conscious mind. They will no longer affect you in any way. You will be able to simply watch them come and go.

In order to do Samatha meditation, you sit in a comfortable cross-legged position (if sitting on the mat is uncomfortable for you, you can also sit on a chair and practice) on the mat, close your eyes, and ensure to you back straight.

Don't force yourself in any particular position and make appropriate adjustments to comfort yourself. If you are not relaxed, you will not be able to meditate.

Start by watching the movement of the breath in and out of your body. Don't force your breath and try to maintain a steady rhythm.

While practicing meditation your mind will keep wandering away to random thoughts every now and then. Whenever that happens just bring your awareness back to your breath gently. Don't feel bad if you are not able to keep your attention on your breath for a sustained period. That happens to everybody in the beginning.

Slowly with time and practice, the wandering of your overactive mind reduces significantly, and as a result, you start feeling calmer and more relaxed. A calm mind helps in developing more clarity and improves decision-making. It makes us kinder and more compassionate towards ourselves and also towards other people.

Samatha is a stage where you understand the connection between your mind and the body. It helps you to clear your mind and liberate yourself from stress, anxiety, and depression. Eventually, it prepares you for a higher stage of meditation known as the Vipassana, where you start developing insight.

Loving Kindness Meditation (LKM)

Also known as the 'Metta' meditation, the Loving-kindness meditation technique allows us to develop feelings of compassion, forgiveness, love, and kindness towards everyone, including ourselves, and even towards those who have been unkind to us. It is especially helpful in cases where you feel hurt by troubled relationships, and there are feelings of anger, resentment, and revenge towards others. It is not easy, and it requires some time for your mind to adapt to this type of contemplation.

Initially, you may feel that you're not able to generate feelings of love and compassion – especially towards people who have been unkind to you. After getting accustomed to the practice of Love-Kindness Mediation, you'll notice that your heart will automatically start opening, and you will begin to feel unconditional love and compassion for others.

We usually get so caught up in day-to-day life that we never, even for a moment, think about the impact of our actions on others.

Our heart is the center of infinite love and compassion, and it keeps radiating loving energy all the time, but our restless mind blocks that radiating energy. Most people with a restless mind are neither able to give nor receive this love and kindness, mainly because they are trapped by their minds that keep them juggling between unproductive thinking and activities that don't matter.

A study[1] published by the Harvard Review of Psychiatry shows that the compassion-based interventions (CBI) and loving-kindness meditation (LKM) can help in treating people with:

- Psychotic disorders.
- Eating disorders.
- Depression.
- Post-traumatic stress disorder,
- and more.

LKM especially is believed to be highly effective in dealing with chronic pain. Although the results have been very encouraging, further studies are needed to confirm these results. It has its origin in Buddhism, and the buddha taught it as a means to develop altruistic love. The pressure of modern-day living has made our minds so numb that we have lost all touch with our emotional states.

LKM helps us recognize feelings of love and compassion, not just for others but also for ourselves. It enables us to practice forgiveness and develop selflessness.

Loving-kindness meditation practice enables us to develop four qualities of love:

- **Friendliness** – also known as the metta, is about cultivating pleasant feelings for others. These can either be someone known or a stranger. Metta can also be cultivated towards other beings like plants, pets, and other animals.

• **Compassion** – the friendliness transforms into compassion for others, where people learn to understand and empathize with people in troubled situations. The Sanskrit word for compassion is 'Karuna.'

• **Joy** – Developing empathy brings about an appreciative joy towards others. Irrespective of how the other person is, you create an emotional harmony within yourself.

• **Equanimity** (upekkha or upeksha) – keeping calm and composure in stressful situations. At this stage, you gain complete control over your emotional states. Even in the most challenging conditions, you successfully evoke unconditional love.

Steps to Practice Loving-Kindness Meditation

This meditation practice works by generating a feeling of love and kindness for:

• People you deeply respect and regard. For example, your teacher, spiritual master, your mentor at work, or someone who has had a high impact on your life.

• A loved one, such as your spouse, parent, child, close friend, or a romantic relationship.

• General acquaintances, like the janitor in your office, server in the restaurant you often visit, the cashier at the supermarket store, etc. These people are neutral towards you. They are neither pleasant nor rude.

• And finally, the unpleasant people. Including those who abused you mentally (or physically) in the past, like a narcissistic ex, toxic parent, manipulative relative, or a rude boss. Don't be in a hurry to go through this step if you are a beginner in LKM.

It takes some time to get used to the LKM practice. While it's easy to generate feelings of love for our family members and close ones, doing the same for others is not easy.

We unknowingly cultivate a lot of negativities towards people who are not a part of our immediate family, but these are people with who we interact regularly. These could be our friends, co-workers, distant relatives, or general acquaintances. Some of these people may not be very pleasant to talk to, or even be downright rude. Therefore, we often start gossiping and criticizing them.

Over time this develops into a habit that clouds the real source of love and happiness within us, and when that happens, it becomes difficult to generate compassion from within. With regular practice, we learn to open up our hearts and allow the love to flow for all beings unconditionally.

Steps to practice loving-kindness meditation (for beginners) are as follows:

1. Find a beautiful and quiet place where you will not be interrupted for the next 5 to 10 minutes.

2. Sit in a comfortable posture of your choice: kneeling position, easy seated pose, or sit on a chair. No matter which posture you choose, ensure that your spine is straight. Feel free to use support (like for the lower back or legs) in case of any discomfort.

3. Ensure that you are comfortable.

4. Close your eyes and bring your awareness to this present moment.

5. Now repeat some positive affirmations for yourself, like "I am safe," "I am secure," "I am healthy," "I am ready to give love and kindness," "I am ready to receive love and kindness." Feel free to come up with your affirmations if

you like.

6. Keep repeating the affirmations for a few minutes till you start experiencing compassion and restfulness within you. Just take note of the pleasant sensations arising within.

7. Now repeat the same affirmations mentioned above for a loved one—someone very close to you, like a family member.

8. Again, spend a few minutes doing step 7. To make this more effective, visualize the face of the person you're sending love and kindness. Remember that by generating love and affection for others, you're healing your inner self.

9. Now repeat the same exercise for someone who departed on a wrong note. This person could be your ex-spouse, former close friend, or anyone close to you, but does not keep up with you anymore. It is okay to skip this step if you feel extremely triggered or anxious thinking about the past.

For beginners, I do not recommend step 9. Take it slow and steady. With time and practice, you'll know when you're ready for it. The idea is to heal the inner aspects of yourself by creating positive and loving energy for others. True healing occurs when you reach a point where you're able to forgive even those who hurt you. It is not to say that you have to go back to them. For example, if your ex was an unpleasant person, there is no need to get him or her back in your life. Ensuring your physical and psychological safety should always be your priority. But forgiveness is important to heal yourself.

If you harbor feelings of revenge or hate for people who hurt you, it'll hurt you even more than it's hurting them. Those feelings will continuously remind you of the unpleasant situations you were in with them, time and again. Forgive and move on. By generating love and kindness for others, we start moving close to the very source of unconditional love within us. By practicing LKM, we experience healing at the deepest levels of our spiritual self.

Body Scan Meditation

It is sometimes also referred to as progressive relaxation meditation. In this type of meditation, you scan your whole body step by step and identify the areas where the tension is building up, and gently allow it to leave. Body scan mediation is beneficial for people suffering from chronic pain and inflammation. It helps them de-stress, relax the body, reduce the effects of pain, and allow for better sleep. This meditation technique is excellent for getting to your known body and the individual parts that carry tension.

You can perform simple experiments and notice the benefits for yourself. The next time you have discomforts like headaches or body pain, perform a body scan around that area.

Try to identify the location of discomfort, acknowledge the existence of pain at that location, notice your reaction to the distress, and release it. Let it go out of the body. Body scan meditation, a variation of mindfulness meditation, is nothing but a simple visualization exercise that helps in dealing with discomforts like pain and inflammation in the body.

Initially, this might seem unscientific and fantasy stuff, but recent studies[2] show that this meditation practice can help reduce chronic stress associated with pain. Many people believe this to be just a placebo effect, but what's the harm if it works.

Vipassana Meditation

Vipassana meditation is an advanced meditation practice and is generally not recommended for beginners because it entails a long time of sitting (as compared to mindfulness meditation) in traditional meditation postures. However, this is one of the most powerful techniques and is known to develop the power of "insight." And insight brings wisdom and maturity.

What that means is that this meditation enables us to see things as they are. Let me explain. In our regular daily lives, we see and judge events based on our perspectives, i.e., the inputs that we gather through the five senses are translated and given a special meaning in our mind based on past conditioning.

It's as if we have created a special filter within our minds. So, whatever information we gather through our senses has to pass through that filter, which, in turn, distorts the information and hides the reality from us. And that is one reason why we evoke unpleasant emotions.

For example, it's common to see some people holding strong prejudices against a particular race or an ethnic group. It generally happens in two kinds of scenarios:

- When someone experiences abuse from members of a particular group or race, or
- When we get conditioned to think negatively by our parents, friends, associations, and society in general. In such cases, the information that reaches you is distorted, and the filter of your mind distorts it even further.

The filters of bias cloud our ability to see reality, and we often resort to acts of aggression and violence against the particular race or group in question. Vipassana reduces (if not eliminate completely) the effects of such conditioning or the filters of mind and gives us the capability to see things as they are. We begin to gain control over our emotions in the most challenging situations. The vision of our mind's eye widens as our consciousness expands. It's not that we lose our ability to perform critical analysis, but we do it with the most compassion in our hearts. When we see things as they are, we do not behave impulsively, our fears and insecurities do not affect our ability to analyze a particular situation.

Thereby, we gain firm control over our thoughts and emotions. Before starting vipassana, it is better if you have some prior experience of sitting in meditation.

If your mind is too restless, you should first practice Samatha - the mindfulness meditation technique based on developing concentration. Here we maintain our focus on a single object such as a candle flame, a deity statue, chanting mantra, or simply the breath.

Vipassana requires you to start by focusing on the movement of the breath. Simply watching how the flow of breath calms down both the body and the mind.

This state of restfulness attained during vipassana remains for an extended period, and not only that, but it also gives us a clear glimpse into the nature of our mind. When the mind slows down sufficiently, it allows you to go deep and witness your thoughts and emotions. The alluring and delightful effects of vipassana last for a long time as compared to other meditation techniques.

Vipassana begins with concentration, using the breath as the anchor, as an instrument that helps to transcend from conscious to the subconscious. Once we go deeper into our minds, the instrument is no longer required. The deeper we go, the more awareness we experience. It gives us knowledge of the "self" slowly and gradually until we reach a stage where the experience and the experiencer become one. Where the witness and object being witnessed, merges. This state is called samadhi, a state of existence (or call it non-existence, if you wish) beyond waking, dreaming, and deep sleep.

When sitting in vipassana for long periods, we begin to notice the impermanence of life. Just like the objects of our experience, such as thoughts and emotions, are temporary, so are the situations, and the whole of physical existence itself. We understand that our ego traps us into the vicious cycle of cause and effect by creating an emotional attachment with the objects of desire. Since no object that we possess has infinite existence, we experience pain and suffering after its loss.We create a massive void within us that the ego tries to fill by acquiring new objects. And again, we succumb to the same cycle of pleasure and pain that diverts our awareness from the present moment.

While sitting in vipassana, we watch the sensations arising within our bodies. However, the critical point to note here is that these sensations are temporary. They appear, play out, and finally disappear. For example, many people experience intense itching in various parts of the body while sitting in meditation, and there's always an urge to break the posture and itch. However, that does not stop the itching.

When the mind is sufficiently quiet, we get an insight that shows us the actual cause of these sensations. These sensations can be a direct consequence of our cravings, addictions, or a deep hidden psychological trauma. Vipassana subdues the ego by quieting the restless mind. And when the mind is sufficiently trained, we learn how to build a healthy detachment from the objects we crave to possess.

Zen Meditation

The word 'Zen' comes from the Chinese word 'Chan,' which comes from the Sanskrit word 'Dhyana', or a state of meditation. Zen signifies the realization of the interconnected nature of all existence, or what we call absolute reality.

This profound realization can only come when one is truly present in this very moment. This moment unifies everything that is, that has ever been, and that ever will be. Zen is not a religion. It is simply a practice that leads to the realization of the self and the universal consciousness. It provides a method through which the limited consciousness merges with the universal consciousness. Both of these are parts of one whole. It is only the veil of ignorance that creates separation, and we think of ourselves as the individual conscious being.

This realization of the self gives rise to virtues such as unconditional love and compassion for all beings, as you do not see yourself separate from anything in the universe.

Zen Meditation is a part of traditional Buddhist practice, also referred to as 'Zazen'. This type of meditation is quite similar to the mindfulness meditation practice where a great emphasis is on being aware of this very present moment, or the 'now'. However, Zen meditation is a more intense practice that requires great dedication and discipline. Practices like Zen and Vipassana are not done merely for physical health benefits, but to gain a deeper realization of the self. One of the best things about Zen meditation is that it does not require a practitioner to subscribe to a particular doctrine or belief system because the idea is to de-condition the conditioned mind of unproductive thoughts and beliefs.

The process is very scientific and practical and requires the practitioner to verify the results through direct personal experience. That's the reason why Zen meditation involves a lot of patience and perseverance.

Before we get to the actual method of practicing Zen meditation, let me share a small story that gives us an understanding of the nature of this intense practice.

Once a Zen practitioner got disillusioned by his meditation practice, and in great frustration, he approached his master and started complaining. He said, "Master I have failed! I cannot do this anymore!".

Upon hearing these words, the master asked, "What happened? Why are you so upset?". The student replied, "No matter what, I can't get rid of the negative thoughts within my mind. The moment I close my eyes, my mind becomes restless, and no matter how hard I try – I cannot stop them".

The master understood the problem and suggested a little modification in the method of meditation. He asked the student to collect a bowl, some white and black colored pebbles, and place them side by side.

He told the student that every time a negative thought comes to his mind, he should put a black pebble in the bowl, and whenever a positive thought comes, he should put the white pebble in the bowl. And when he's done with the meditation, he should check the bowl to see how many black and white pebbles are there.

For a few months, the bowl remained full of black-colored pebbles. But as time progressed, the bowl started filling with some white-colored pebbles, and then as the time further progressed, the bowl started filling with equal quantities of both black and white pebbles. Finally, after a few years, the bowl had all the white pebbles and just a few black ones. At this stage, the student had fully understood the nature of his mind.

Earlier, he tried to control the negative thoughts, which resulted in his mind becoming even more restless. As soon as the student stopped offering resistance to the mind, it became calmer and more relaxed. As one enters the deep states of mind, both white and black pebbles become irrelevant. The thoughts will always be there, but our reaction to those thoughts is that of a non-judgmental observer, the one who keeps watching the thoughts arise and fall; just like when you look at the traffic outside from the window of your house. You can see the cars entering and leaving your awareness. You are not bothered by the car's attributes, like color, make, model, or who's driving it. Your mind remains calm, and you simply witness the objects (cars) moving in and out of your awareness.

Method of Practicing Zen Meditation (Zazen)

Just like vipassana, zazen is also a very intense practice that requires sitting for long hours. The monks usually get up very early in the morning, somewhere around 3:00 AM. They have to continuously meditate for a specified period, usually about 3 to 4 hours, or even more. It encompasses sitting upright in a good posture (full lotus, half-lotus, or the kneeling pose) and focusing on your breath. For sitting, we use a meditation cushion, known as the Zafu.

The Zafu ensures that your hips are higher than the knees, taking off the pressure from the knees. It also helps in maintaining the spine erect. Sometimes a rectangular matt is also placed below the Zafu to provide cushioning to the lower part of the body. It is known as the Zabuton. Ensure that your back and neck are straight, and your ears are in alignment with the shoulders. It not only prevents injury but also enhances the meditation experience. It will also stop you from getting drowsy and dosing off to sleep. Your mouth should be closed, and the tongue should be touching the roof of the mouth with the tip aligned with the inner side of the front teeth.

The eyes should be in a half-opened state, and the gaze should be about 1 meter in the front. The traditional Zen meditation requires your eyes to be open; however, you can also keep them closed, if you wish. The hands should be on top of one another. The left hand should be on top of the right one so that the palms are visible to you. The thumbs should be touching at the tips forming an oval shape. This arrangement of the hands is known as the *cosmic mudra*. Refer to the image shown below.

First, notice the in-flow of your breath as it travels from your nostrils and reaches your belly, causing it to expand a little, and after that, notice the outflow, all the way from belly to the nostrils, from where the breath exits the body. Keep paying attention to your breath till you start feeling sufficiently relaxed. There will be moments when you are likely to get distracted by the thoughts arising in your mind, distorting the oval structure of the hands.

Whenever that happens, just gently bring your awareness back to your breathing. Don't be tense or worried about the progress. Over time your mind will start becoming more and more aware, and the distracting thoughts will reduce. If you're a beginner, you should practice this meditation for a short duration of time - say 15 to 20 minutes max. You can time yourself using the timer app on your smartphone. When finished, don't be in a hurry to get up, take your time, and move gently.

Practices like zazen and vipassana are usually not done in isolation. Since they entail long hours of sitting without moving the body, it's better to practice these types of meditations in group-like settings. It is better to practice zazen under the supervision of an expert Zen teacher. There are various retreats all across the world that offer time-limited courses if you'd like to practice vipassana or zazen. For regular folks like us, there are short duration courses, for like 4 to 10 days or so.

Transcendental Meditation (TM)

Transcendental meditation (also referred to as TM) finds its origin in the Vedic scriptures, and it was popularized in the West by Maharishi Mahesh Yogi in the 1960s. To popularize TM, Maharishi started conducting a huge number of classes and started training people to teach TM to the general population. The craze for transcendental meditation grew to such heights that even the most popular celebrities started practicing TM.

Even today, celebrities like Jennifer Aniston, Hugh Jackman, and Oprah Winfrey, vouch for the benefits of this simple meditation technique. To understand how transcendental meditation works, we go back to the ocean analogy discussed in the earlier section. Imagine yourself stranded in the middle of an ocean, trapped in a storm. On the surface, you will witness extremely violent waves that will make you very anxious and sacred.

Now imagine that you are transported to the bottom of the ocean using a submarine. You will witness that the bottom of the ocean is always quiet. No matter how violent the waves are at the surface, the bottom is always peaceful. You can see that clearly because you're looking at the complete cross-section of the ocean. Whereas earlier, you thought that the surface of the ocean was the only reality.

And it is the main reason for our suffering. In our daily lives, our mind is constantly thinking, and these thoughts are just like the violent wave at the surface of the ocean. But practicing transcendental meditation, we gradually start experiencing restfulness, as if something has magically transported us to the bottom of the ocean. The practice is quite similar to other meditation techniques, except that one has to silently repeat a mantra instead of focusing on the breath.

Repeating the mantra, again and again, we transcend the ordinary state of mind, which is like the ocean's surface, violent and restless. This transcendence takes one into the most restful state of mind or pure consciousness. For best results, it is recommended that you practice the TM for at least 20 minutes, both in the morning and evening.

Transcendental meditation is an effortless meditation technique that does not require us to control or manipulate our mind using either focus or concentration techniques. However, let me emphasize that no meditation requires us to control the mind as such. Anybody who tries to control the mind during meditation is bound to fail miserably. The mind is too powerful to be controlled. The moment you try to control the mind, it will offer the worst possible resistance. The mantra used in transcendental meditation serves as an anchor, just like the breath, that enables (or rather tricks) us to reach the vast depths of the mind where everything is calm and peaceful.

Kundalini Yoga Meditation

The word kundalini comes from the Sanskrit word kundal, which means a curl. Kundalini is the psychic energy that flows within our spiritual body. In the majority of people, this energy lies in a dormant state and at the base of the spine. This energy is generally depicted as a serpent because it lies coiled up in its place of rest – which is the root chakra.

Awakening of this energy is a very transformational experience for an individual. As this energy rises, hitting the different energy points along the way, it marks a significant change in the practitioner's consciousness. Awakening of kundalini is a powerful experience. You should not take it lightly. It's better to seek proper guidance and have a clear-cut understanding of this process before you attempt the kundalini yoga practice. You should seek guidance from an expert master who can guide and give a step-by-step process of practicing this meditation technique.

Practices like yoga and meditation stimulate this primordial energy. It starts moving upwards from the base of the spine to the top of the head where it merges with the cosmic energy.

Introduction to the Chakras

Now I'm going to introduce you to the concept of chakras. Chakras are the energy points within our spiritual body stimulated by the flow of the kundalini energy. The flow of energy in and out of these chakras governs our existence's physical and psychological aspects. Kundalini energy helps balance these chakras; what it means is that the flow of energy in and out of a chakra should be optimal.

A chakra that has less energy flowing through it is said to be underactive, which translates into physical, mental, and other types of ailments. Whereas, a chakra that has excessive energy flowing through it, is said to be overactive and has its own set of associated problems. Therefore, to attain physical, mental, financial, and spiritual wellness, one should balance the energy flow within all the seven chakras. And when this happens, the chakras are said to be in alignment. I am going to introduce you to the seven chakras briefly, but I'm not going to go into details, because I have already written extensively about them on this website. If you want more information, I will provide the appropriate links for each chakra. According to the kundalini yoga practice, there are seven psycho-spiritual points (chakras) within our ethereal body. They are as follows.

Root Chakra

The root chakra, also known as the Muladhara chakra, is the very first chakra of our spiritual body that is associated with stability, vitality, security, and fulfillment of our material needs like food, water, and shelter. People who struggle with their finances usually have an out-of-balance root chakra. If you are the kind of person who puts in a lot of hard work but cannot transform efforts into payouts, you need to work on your root chakra.

Symptoms of the blocked root chakra are as follows:

1. Having lots of fears and insecurities.
2. Suffering from codependency.
3. Dysfunctional relationships.
4. Having trust issues with people.
5. Unable to focus.
6. Having problems in the lower parts of your body like lower back pain, constipation, bladder, kidneys, etc.

If you would like to learn more about root and higher chakra healing, you can check out my website mindfulnessquest.com.

Sacral Chakra

The sacral chakra is the second chakra of the spiritual body associated with pleasure, wellness, abundance, sensuality, confidence, and joy. The sacral chakra has a connection with our subconscious mind, which is the center of infinite creative potential. This chakra is located near the genitals region and is said to be the source of our creation.

Symptoms of blockage in the sacral chakra are as follows:

1. Lack of confidence.
2. Lack of creativity.
3. Inability to control emotions.

4. Lack of sexual desire.
5. Fear of physical and emotional intimacy.
6. Excessive daydreaming.
7. Addiction to substances.

Solar Plexus Chakra

Solar plexus, aka the Manipura chakra, is associated with self-development, personal growth, transformation, and self-confidence. If you are the kind of person who dreams big, makes exciting plans, formulates goals, but fails when it comes to taking action, your solar plexus chakra is blocked.

Some other symptoms of blocked solar plexus chakra are as follows:

1. Low self-esteem.
2. Daydreaming.
3. Always feeling like a victim.
4. Lack of self-discipline.
5. Stubborn attitude.
6. Need to control others.
7. Suffer from anxiety.

Heart Chakra

The heart chakra is the fourth chakra of the spiritual body that is said to be "the seat of the soul". It is associated with kindness, compassion, forgiveness, and unconditional love.

A few symptoms of heart chakra blockage are as follows:

1. Holding grudges with people.
2. Gossiping and criticizing people behind their backs.
3. Commitment issues.
4. Unable to forgive others.
5. Feelings of resentment and anger.

Throat Chakra

The throat chakra is associated with purity of thought, the ability to express clearly, and the sharpening of the mind. People with open throat chakra are excellent speakers and have robust communication skills. They are fearless when it comes to expressing their thoughts and ideas. They never suppress their true feelings. And at the same time, they're also good listeners. They do not interrupt others and have high compassion for all living beings.

Third Eye Chakra

The third eye chakra (or Ajna) is the center of spiritual awakening and higher consciousness. The third eye is the point where one gains the power of higher intuition and supreme knowledge. The third eye is the gateway to divine knowledge. This is not the regular knowledge that one attains through the intellect.

It is an "instant knowing" in the form of intuition. At this point, all the concepts of duality dissolve, and 'oneness' with the universe is experienced. For more information on the third chakra, please read my article on awakening the third chakra.

Crown Chakra

Crown chakra is the final chakra that lies on top of the head, and it is a point at which the individual consciousness merges with the supreme universal consciousness. Awakening the crown chakra leads to higher wisdom, peace, tranquility, and unlimited love.

Kundalini Awakening

Once again, kundalini awakening is a very intense experience, and one must be fully prepared, physically, and mentally, before undertaking this journey. It completely changes the way we see this world. Once your kundalini is awakened, you will never be the same person again. You will see this universe as one whole that manifests itself as many.

Benefits of Kundalini Awakening

It's not that awakening the kundalini - you will become an ascetic and run off to the Himalayas, breaking all bonds with worldly things. No. It's quite the opposite. Here's what will happen.

- You will be more conscious of all actions that you perform.
- You will resonate with high frequency.
- You will draw positive energies towards you.
- You will be more grounded and more aware.
- You will be more mindful while making decisions about work and life.
- You would be more loving and compassionate towards those who are still asleep.
- You will learn to create a harmonious balance between your material and spiritual life.

Yogic Sleep Meditation (Yoga Nidra)

Yogic sleep meditation is a conscious sleep-inducing meditation technique that promotes deep relaxation and offers many benefits. The Sanskrit word for it is Yoga Nidra, which is a semi-conscious sleep state, also known as psychic sleep. For many years, I was unknowingly practicing yogic sleep. Doing Shavasana (the corpse pose) was a routine practice after performing strenuous yoga exercises. It usually is the last posture we practice to relax the body. In fact, most yoga teachers put great emphasis on ending a good yoga session with Shavasana.

While others practiced Shavasana for about 2 to 5 minutes, I used to go beyond that time limit. Sometimes, up to 40 to 50 minutes, because it felt so good. Believe it or not, it significantly improved my night's sleep. Later on, I realized that this is the powerful yogic sleep, also known as the Yoga Nidra practice. It came naturally to me. Yogic sleep is a yoga practice that is extremely beneficial for physical and mental wellbeing. Yogic sleep makes you enter into a deep state of awareness as the brainwaves begin to slow down and the mind progressively becomes restful. This experience is quite similar to that of deep meditation, but the process is gradual, and it takes time to get comfortable with it.

It comprises the body, breath, and awareness techniques that transform the thinking (high brainwave) state of mind into the calm (low brainwave) state, which is usually experienced as the state of simply 'being.' It is an effortless practice that helps develop inner awareness.

Some of the benefits of Yogic Sleep are as follow:

- Helps in decreasing stress and anxiety.
- Improves the quality of sleep.
- Helps in reducing chronic stress and combats PTSD.
- Helps in chronic pain.
- Increases awareness.
- Improves focus and concentration.

- Helps in getting rid of bad habits, including addictions.
- Calms the mind.
- Improvement in learning ability.
- Develops clarity in thinking.

In a recent study, scientists explored the benefits of yogic sleep on sixty college professors. This study's duration was three months, and the psychological variables included stress, anxiety, and depression. The college professors comprising men and women were divided into three experimental groups: Yogic sleep, seated meditation, and control group. The results showed that Yoga Nidra had a greater tendency towards reducing stress and anxiety.

Yogic sleep provides us with the restorative benefits of normal sleep in less time. However, don't attempt to replace your normal sleep with yogic sleep; otherwise, you will fall asleep during the practice. Your mind and body need restorative sleep for healthy functioning.

Yogic sleep helps to clear the mental blockages in a very subtle manner. When practiced consistently, it reprograms the subconscious mind, and therefore, this ancient technique serves as a powerful mechanism for clearing psychic scars and deep traumas.

Difference Between Yogic Sleep, Meditation, and Restorative Sleep?

Meditation practice requires sitting still in traditional yoga postures like the easy pose, sukhasana, or the lotus pose. However, most people lack the flexibility to sit in these complicated poses. When the body is in discomfort, it's hard to calm down the mind, and as a result, traditional meditation techniques are sometimes not apt for absolute beginners. That is where the yogic sleep technique proves effective. Yogic sleep is also a meditation practice, but since it requires you to lie down and sleep, it's much easier than traditional meditation practices.

However, sleep is semi-conscious, i.e., you retain your conscious awareness at all times. This semi-conscious state prevents you from drifting into sleep, but at the same time, it relaxes your senses. During normal restorative sleep, we close our eyes, and as soon as the mind slows down, we slip into the unconscious without any awareness of what's happening around us. However, in yogic sleep, we are in a conscious or semi-conscious state, fully aware of what's happening inside, and allow the healing messages to seep into the subconscious.

It is a dream-like state, but at the same time, we're aware of what's happening around us. We can hear sounds, and yet we're not disturbed by them at any time. That's why we call yogic sleep conscious sleep.

Yogic sleep is easy to learn because sleeping or relaxing is a natural phenomenon. We don't have to make an effort to sleep (unless we are suffering from insomnia).

But that said, during the Yoga Nidra sessions, your mind is very likely to drift into unconscious sleep as it gets more relaxed. This is normal for beginners, so don't get disheartened.

Whenever you feel you're falling asleep, bring back your awareness and continue with the Nidra. This is similar to what we do in traditional meditation. Over time, you train your mind to remain conscious during yogic sleep. In meditation, the practitioner has to start by focusing on the object of meditation, which can be the breath, sound, a physical object (such as a candle), or a mantra that you recite mentally to facilitate the transition from the conscious to the subconscious.

You need not concentrate on the breath or any singular object to facilitate this transition in yogic sleep. The state that is required for Yoga Nidra is somewhere between the conscious and subconscious mind where the senses are very lightly engaged. This state is easily achieved within a few minutes in practice, whereas, in traditional meditation, it requires some practice before you can access a deep psychological state.

How to Practice Yoga Nidra in Four Easy Steps

Get started by lying down on a mat in Shavasana (the corpse pose). Ensure that the surface is soft and that you're lying down in a comfortable position. Feel free to place a soft cushion below your knees or lower back if required. Close your eyes and relax.

1. Setting the Intention – think about why you're doing this. There may be a blocked feeling, emotion, or an unfulfilled desire that may be causing unhappiness in your life. Whatever it is, you need to accept it and set an intention to relax.

2. Bring awareness to your breath – the breath, or prana, in yogic terminology, is the life-force energy that sustains the mind-body complex. By bringing our awareness to the breath and increasing the flow of prana, we relax our nervous system. Slowly as time passes, the mind slows down, and the restfulness starts increasing.

3. Be aware of the bodily sensations – Notice the sensations arising within the body. We scan the entire body, starting from the feet and finishing at the top of the head. We let go of any tension or stress build-up in any

part of the body. If there is an uncomfortable sensation, we first observe (by bringing awareness) the area of sensation, allow the sensation to play out, and finally, release it.

4. Be aware of your thoughts and feelings – once the body is sufficiently relaxed, we start experiencing random thoughts accompanied by some troubling emotions, like anxiety, anger, worry, and restlessness. Watch these emotions play out and let them go. By releasing these afflicting emotions, we clear out the subconscious of the negative energy.

Once finished, slowly open your eyes, sit down, and reflect upon your experience. For beginners, ten to fifteen minutes is enough. Initially, this might be a little hard as the mind is not conditioned, but over time, as your mind becomes calm, you will begin to experience deep relaxation.

Walking Meditation

This can be a wonderful option for all the busy folks out there. Walking is something everyone can do. It doesn't take much effort and you can always spare time for it. In fact, walking meditation if done right can become your deep spiritual practice. In walking meditation, we walk slowly and take each step with full awareness and mindfulness. We keep our bodies relaxed and take deep breathes before starting to walk. We take notice of how our legs touch the ground one after the other. Avoid taking sharp or sudden turns.

Just like with all other meditations while practicing walking meditation we also generate thoughts. Whenever we find ourselves lost in these thoughts, we bring our attention back to the steps. It's also better to practice conscious breathing while walking.

Deep Meditative Experience

When we sit for meditation, our mind gets tangled in random thoughts, and at times, we feel completely lost. After a few minutes, when we open our eyes, we feel that we wasted the entire session and didn't make any progress. For me, it was a long period of struggle and frustration. I did not have access to proper guidance at that time. Once you get the fundamentals right, you significantly shorten the learning curve and experience a blissful state during meditation.

As I have always said in my earlier posts, meditation is like running a marathon and not a sprint. So don't expect quick results. It generally takes a long time to condition your mind to get into a deep meditative state.

If you want to experience deep meditation, you should be willing to spend a little more time than usual. I'd recommend that you devote at least 45 minutes to 1 hour of your time every day. Getting to experience deep meditation is a process, and it required time and practice. There will be many times when you will face disappointment. But don't give up.

As of now, your mind is conditioned to behave in a particular way. It is like a child who is restless and full of energy. Therefore, it likes to wander now and then. This is also known as the monkey mind. It takes time and patience to tame the monkey mind, so don't expect this to happen overnight. Depending on how dedicated you are to your practice, it can take a few days, weeks, months, or even years. Before starting your meditation, it is better to relax your body and mind. I know what you are thinking. But doesn't meditation do that? And yes, it does, but our goal here is not just to relax but to go deep into the experience.

We start by doing a breathing exercise known as pranayama in eastern cultures. It's an ancient Indian practice that teaches us a simple technique to master the breath. This exercise reduces stress and anxiety and makes your meditation more enjoyable and transformative. You can either sit on a chair or sit on the ground in a cross-legged position. Whichever way suits you. Take deep breaths maintaining the natural flow. Observe the sensation of air moving in and out of the nostrils.

As you exhale, try and relax your muscles and let go of any tension and stress build up inside your body. This exercise prepares your mind and body for meditation and can be done for about 5 to 10 minutes. Next, for a couple of minutes, just be seated and ground yourself. Try to be aware of what's happening around you and observe any sensation arising in your body. Try listening to your heartbeat, chirping birds, watching the color of the sky, and if you are sitting out in the open, feel the flow of air on your body.

If you still feel the tension in some areas like the neck or back, do some simple stretches to let go of the tension in that particular area. Every meditation starts with concentration and focus. We focus on our breathing or chant a mantra, and whenever we get distracting thoughts, we use a little bit of willpower to bring our attention back to our meditation method. After a few minutes, we go into a deep state of mind, where we experience absolute stillness and perfect silence. Whenever you experience this silence, you will know that you have reached deep in your meditation.

At this point, you don't need to concentrate anymore or apply willpower to maintain yourself in that state. There will be absolutely nothing. Even the sense of 'I' is lost. It's hard to describe that state.

The best I can express in words is that it feels like a merging of nothing with the vastness of everything. As one merges with the vastness, the personal sense of 'I' disappears, and what remains is the infinite awareness or pure love.

[1] https://journals.lww.com/hrpjournal/Abstract/2018/07000/Compassion_and_Loving_Kindness_Meditation__An.3.aspx

[2] https://pubmed.ncbi.nlm.nih.gov/28961631/

CHAPTER FIVE

ANSWERS TO FREQUENTLY ASKED QUESTIONS ON MEDITATION

I often get bombarded with questions regarding mindfulness and meditation. Sometimes these are repetitive, so I decided to create this section where I answer some of the most commonly asked questions.

How Meditation Helps in Dealing with Stress and Anxiety?

We have already discussed the scientific benefits of practicing meditation in the second chapter. Now we'll get into the spiritual aspect that deals with the root of all psychological ailments. What you appear on the outside is a reflection of your inner-self. A stressful mind will create unpleasantness in every aspect of life, from work to relationships. Therefore, real healing starts with the inner-self. The reason why we feel stressed and anxious is that we start building strong identifications with a particular group of thoughts that repeat over and over again in our minds.

The stronger this identification becomes, the more our mind becomes restless, and stress is an effect of that which we feel like a symptom in the physical body.

Practices like mindfulness and meditation teach us how to break the powerful grip of these identifications. It is a challenging endeavor. Why? Because we have been unconsciously building identifications all our life.

Some of the examples of such identifications are as follows:

- Strong identifications with culture, religious beliefs, or social groups.
- Strong identification with the color of the skin or gender.
- Strong identification with preferences of art and music.
- Strong identification with personal beliefs.
- Strong identification with caste, creed, sect, or organization.

Our environment and childhood conditioning have a very significant effect on the types of identifications we build, so much so, that we become anxious (or even aggressive), the moment anybody even slightly challenges our beliefs. We have become so identified with our personal beliefs that we start creating strong biases towards other ideas and beliefs. This eventually results in feelings of discontent, prejudice, and even hate. The afflicting thoughts generated as a result, constantly bother us and sink into our subconscious mind. As a result, we become slaves of our own minds.

That's why we see some people in religion, politics, business, and even academia, behaving like fanatics at times—losing all of our capacity to think rationally. It's because we start associating our sense of self with our identifications.

For example, if I make a statement that "you're a horrible worker in your profession", some of you will be extremely offended because you have built strong identifications around your work and the position you hold in your organization. But does my saying that makes it a fact? In fact, just notice the absurdity of the above statement. What does "horrible worker" even mean? But the problem is that once we are triggered, we won't have any capacity to logically analyze the above statement.

A stressful mind will always react rather than respond to criticisms. It's because we have unconsciously trained ourselves to do that, and now it has become a pattern of behavior. Human beings have a tendency to unconsciously expose their triggers and vulnerabilities. That makes it easy for other people to exploit and control us. And that creates even more stress.

Meditation creates a gap, or a short window of time, where it gives us the option to choose our action. It gives us the opportunity to respond instead of reacting to criticism. It also gives us the option to disengage from the situation by not allowing the ego to take over. Another case of identification with thoughts is when we keep revisiting unpleasant incidents of the past. Sometimes the imprints of such incidents are so deep that they keep us trapped for a long time.

And then there are times we worry thinking about the future. These patterns of thoughts grow stronger as we engage more and more with them. This constant juggling between multiple thoughts creates restlessness and unhappiness. Mindfulness and meditation teach our minds to remain in the present moment. It's not that we have to forcefully try to block our thoughts. We simply allow them to arise, play, and then disappear, without getting involved.

While the thoughts are playing in mind, we simply watch them without creating any kind of reaction or judgment. Meditation heightens our awareness and gives us the ability to watch our minds.

How Do I Know Which Meditation Practice is Best for Me?

What type of meditation practice is suitable for you depends on your personality and the kind of belief structure you hold. For example, if you are someone with an extremely restless mind, I would not suggest Vipassana or Zen meditation in the initial phase.

The first step is to train your mind to concentrate. We have to teach ourselves to relax before we go deep within the mind. To do that, we must be mindful of the food we eat and the kind of content we consume. If you're the kind of person who compulsively keeps checking email, watches random videos, or obsessively scrolls social media feeds to distract yourself from underlying thoughts and feelings. It's apparent that you have an anxious brain and are addicted to high dopamine release. In such cases, you need to do some introspection and ask yourself, why do you behave in this manner, and how is this behavior helping you to move closer to your life goals.

Besides following a healthy lifestyle, which in my opinion is of high importance, it would help if you got started by practicing the breathing exercises mentioned in the second chapter. These exercises will help you relax your body and set the right conditions to practice meditation. If you find it hard to close your eyes and sit in meditation all by yourself, you can practice either walking meditation or listening to a guided meditation track.

Guided meditation tracks are okay to listen to if you're an absolute beginner, but they are not as beneficial as the traditional meditation practices in the long run. Another option would be to practice Japa, or mantra meditation, where you keep chanting a mantra repeatedly until the mind becomes quiet. You either say the mantra aloud or repeat it silently in your mind. Using the Japa mala beads can help you to build concentration in your meditation session. As you gain more control over your mind, try out advanced forms of meditation practices such as Vipassana.

What is the Best Time to Practice Meditation?

Although meditation can be practiced anytime and anyplace, it's most beneficial to practice meditation during the morning hours, the reason being that at that time you are well rested after a good night's sleep, and the mind is most relaxed. However, this is not a hard and fast rule. For example, I like to practice meditation both in the morning and evening and sometimes also during mid-day.

If you like to meditate in the evenings, and for long durations, ensure that you don't do it very close to the time you go to sleep. If you meditate for more than an hour just before sleeping, it might interfere with your sleep. For short durations, like 5 to 10 minutes, it's not a problem.

What Type of Foods Are Best for Meditation?

According to ayurvedic classification, there are three types of foods:

- **Sattva** – the most balanced diet that creates perfect harmony between the body and mind. Traditionally, this is considered to be the best diet for yoga and meditation practitioners.
- **Rajas** – this diet is stimulating in nature, like tea and coffee. It's not bad. It's just that consuming too much of it may make you overexcited or even anxious, at times. Eating it in moderation will not be a problem.
- **Tamas** – this type of diet creates laziness and lathery within the body. The items include high carbohydrate and sugary foods, like sodas, cakes, pastries, fried foods, etc.

If you want details, you can check my article eight Sattvic Foods[1] for Healthy Body and Mind on my website mindfulnessquest.com. The only thing that you should take care of is that there should be some gap (preferably 1 hour or more) between your last meal, and the time you practice meditation.

If you start meditating immediately after eating a meal, you will not be able to focus on your breathing or mantra recitation, because organs in your body will be busy digesting the food you ate, but that said, you should also not be starving.

What is the Difference Between Meditation and Concentration?

I see a lot of people confused between meditation and concentration. Meditation begins with concentration only to quiet the mind and slips into watchfulness afterward. The idea is to stay with watchfulness for the duration of meditation. This watchfulness doesn't have any particular characteristics. It is simply watching whatever arises in the mind with a non-reactive and non-judgmental awareness.

We use anchors like the breath, sound, or mantra, only to allow the mind to settle down. If the mind is agitated, the state where the mind can observe itself will not be possible. An agitated mind will never let you experience blissful calm. Therefore, it's better to start your meditation by concentrating on an object, keeping awareness on that object till the mind settles down, and then letting go of the object by entering into a state of watchfulness. If you treat meditation purely as a concentration exercise, it will be no different than any other activity like singing, dancing, painting, etc. In fact, it may lead to greater frustration when the mind is unable to maintain focus.

This is where a lot of western people struggle. They have been so trained to be focus-oriented that it's difficult for them to let go of control. They start evaluating and comparing their performance. It is a recipe for disaster. You're harming yourself when you practice meditation like that. Some people are obsessed with the duration of their meditation sessions. They boast about it. They feel proud that they can sit for long hours. In fact, I've seen a few teachers organizing X days meditation challenges for their students. This is nonsense.

The duration of your meditation is insignificant. It's all about being in the state of watchfulness that I described above. Watchfulness for 10 minutes will be more beneficial than sitting in concentration for 1 hour.

Meditation is for clearing the mind. All that has to be done is cleaning, but you think of becoming a better cleaner, you're back into the trap of ego. The real meditation happens when the meditator disappears and all that remains is watchful awareness.

Is Meditation a Selfish Activity?

I hear a lot about how meditation is a selfish activity. What are we accomplishing sitting with our eyes closed when there's so much to do out there?

You see, any activity can become a selfish activity, including meditation. When the meditation is done to become a good meditator, it is the ego that is feeding itself by thinking that it's achieving a milestone. Real meditation happens when the meditator disappears. Till there is someone sitting with his or her eyes closed, in a perfectly seated posture, chanting the ancient sacred mantras, the meditation is not happening.

Therefore, meditation is the absence of the person unveiling the pure awareness that is our true essence. Hence, meditation is only selfless activity, subject to the condition that the meditator disappears in meditation. A meditative mind is a sattvic (harmonious) mind. And we have already established how a calm mind creates positive emotions. Therefore, an emotionally regulated person is a better leader or a decision-maker.

Your radiance of calm and compassion is enough to create the same in others. What have you really achieved by "doing" or medaling in others' affairs? All of your doing creates more problems than it solves. Whether it is at the level of national decisions or personal. When you're anxious, what type of presence do you prefer? Would like to be in the presence of a calm person who patiently listens or would you like to be in the presence of a restless soul that is more eager to give you a bunch of advice that they never applied to themselves.

When Ramana Maharishi was questioned as to why he's wasting time sitting in meditation when there's so much to do in the world, his answer was that it's your assumption that I'm not doing anything.

I Feel Like Meditating but I'm Too Busy and Can't Find Time?

Once, a CEO of a big corporation was attending a meditation retreat in an ashram in India. After the retreat he spoke to the head monk and said that though he liked to meditate, it makes him calm and peaceful, he can't find time out of his busy schedule to practice it on a regular basis.

The monk asked the CEO to accompany him for a walk. He took him to a nearby graveyard and they both kept walking silently for a while. Finally, the CEO asked, why am I here? The monk said, look at all of these people in their graves, once they were all very busy, just like you.

The point is not that you have to do meditation only with a fixed method. But somewhere in the chaos of life, you have to find time to observe your mind.

Doesn't matter what you do. Do meditation, yoga, Japa, or whichever spiritual practice you prefer, but you have to take a pause and reflect on your mind to know yourself. No matter how busy, all of us can find time to meditate for 20 to 30 minutes a week. And if you say that you can't do even that much, then it's just your mind trying to divert your attention. The monkey mind doesn't like to meditate.

What you can do is, tell your mind that I'll meditate for only 2 minutes a week or day. Don't give yourself a daunting task. Trick the mind by under committing. As you begin to experience calmer, the mind will automatically adapt to the routine. Our mind creates the idea of urgency and importance. We easily get hooked on our brain chemistry. There's no dearth of time, but our mind tries to convince us that some things are more important than others. As a result, we neglect our bodies and suffer from ailments.

Meditation brings clarity and helps to see the big picture. We see life as a fragmented reality: work, home, family, business, health, spirituality, and more, and we tend to give too much importance to some aspects over others.

But this imbalance cause problems, and life, in and of itself, is an interconnected whole. For example, you may be successful in your profession, but if your family and relationships are a mess, which is a common case nowadays, you won't be happy. Fulfillment doesn't come from excellence; it comes from balance. A balanced mind is the best mind.

If you feel you're too busy to find time for yourself, go out and observe other busy people, and see how peaceful they are in their daily living. When you learn to be alone by yourself, you discover something immensely valuable. The things that you dislike in yourself are a part of the false image that you've created and nurtured because of the past social and environmental conditioning. They're unreal and have nothing to do with who you really are.

I Feel I've Become Too Sensitive After Practicing Meditation. Why Is That?

This is perfectly normal and happens during one of the stages of meditation. It's a sign that you are doing it right. Think about it. You have been harboring some uncomfortable emotions for years in the depths of your mind. So it's very natural for you to be highly sensitive to them. Don't judge yourself for being sensitive. Realize that this is a superpower.

Sensitivity can be of two types, inner sensitivity, and outer sensitivity. Inner sensitivity is all about your thoughts, feelings, and emotions, whereas outer sensitivity is about the external stimuli which are constantly present at all times, such as sounds and noises of the electronic gadgets around us, lighting in our rooms, and the temperature of the environment in which we live.

From the physical perspective, a highly sensitive person is one who has a high sensory perception capability. People with high sensitivity show a heightened level of awareness of social and environmental stimuli. When we meditate regularly, we become more aware of ourselves and our surroundings, and as a result, our sense perception capability enhances. When you begin meditation one of the first challenges you face is that your mind keeps wandering every now and then, and it's difficult for you to keep yourself focused. With sufficient practice, you start realizing that your conscious mind becomes less cluttered and that the frequency of your mind wandering decreases significantly.

Now as the mind becomes clearer and still, all those hidden feelings and emotions which were lying dormant in your subconscious mind gradually start coming up to the surface of the conscious mind. For a very long time, you have trained yourself to ignore these hidden emotions and feelings. These emotions could be associated with anything like a trauma that occurred early on in your life, feelings of resentment for family or people who are close to you, loss of a loved one, or undergoing abuse or ill-treatment as a child.

Your mind is intelligent and it knows how to suppress these negative feelings and emotions by getting you hooked onto addictions that give short bursts of pleasure, such as drug abuse, playing video games mindlessly for long hours, binge-watching television, binge eating, and drinking alcohol, among other things.

It is very normal for these feelings to come up while meditating. Try to think of this as a cleansing process of the mind. I can understand that these feelings are very uncomfortable and difficult to deal with. They well up like an active volcano that is about to erupt. *Let it flow.*

Accept these feelings and let them pass. With regular meditation practice, a time will come when these feelings and negative emotions associated with them will not bother you anymore. You will simply become an observer who's just watching the contents of the mind, without judging them.

Will Caffeine Intake Affect My Meditation?

The Ayurveda clearly says that coffee is a stimulant and falls under the Rajasic category of foods. Rajasic foods are considered good for enhancing performance, such as in sports or other activities that require pushing the body or mind to its extreme limits. Can meditation and caffeine consumption go together?

Since caffeine is a stimulant, one might feel that it can help focus better in meditation. But my personal experience says that it does not. In fact, the effect is quite the opposite. I would say that it's not much of an issue, but there are certain things you need to understand if you are mixing these two in your daily routine, as they have a very different kind of effect on our mind and body. The thing to understand here is that when I say caffeine, I'm not just referring to that cup of coffee you drink in the morning. Caffeine is present almost everywhere and in everything. It's in your soda drinks, energy-boosting drinks, cakes, and pastries and is in many packed food items.

We keep releasing a chemical called Adenosine, which keeps accumulating in our brain whenever we are awake. The longer we are awake, the more adenosine we collect in the brain. It slows down brain activity and makes us feel tired. When we sleep at night, adenosine concentration steadily declines, and we feel active again in the morning.

Consuming caffeine competes for adenosine receptors in the brain and does not allow adenosine to accumulate in the brain. As a result, our brain cannot signal to the body that it's tired, and that's exactly how we keep going on for hours and hours without getting tired or fatigued. So where's the problem?

The problem is that your brain thinks it requires more adenosine to signal to the body that it's tired. Therefore, it increases the number of receptors to collect more adenosine. To counteract this effect, we tend to consume more coffee to keep awake. That's why when we try to quit coffee, we get horrible withdrawal symptoms like headaches, nausea, tiredness, mood swings, and low energy.

Also, caffeine boosts the production of Adrenaline (the "flight or fight" hormone produced by the body). It increases your heart rate, gets more of your blood pumping, and opens your airways. It affects the dopamine levels in your brain, and as a result, you feel happy and charged up. Meditation works in the opposite way. There is an area in the brain called the PFC (or the Prefrontal Cortex). It is the most evolved part of our brain and greatly influences key executive functions such as decision making, impulse control, reasoning, problem-solving, and creative thinking, among other things.

Recent studies have indicated an increase in the gray matter density in the prefrontal lobe. Studies have also shown a decrease in the size of the Amygdala, a region associated with the "fight or flight" response. Another region of the brain, called the Default Mode Network (or DMN), is sometimes associated with the wandering mind or the "monkey mind." DMN shows increased activity when we keep jumping from one thought to another, and this kind of response is generally associated with unhappiness and dullness. Mindfulness practices have been shown to reduce the Default Mode Network activities. It has been observed that caffeine has an opposite effect to that felt after practicing meditation. Can we mix the two together?

It's not about whether you should have caffeine or not but what is right for you and your body type. If your body gets overstimulated by the consumption of caffeine, you should definitely consider reducing your intake. Avoid drinking sodas and energy-boosting drinks because, first of all, they are not very healthy for you, and secondly, they contain large amounts of caffeine your body can handle. Also, in addition to caffeine, they contain many other things that are not good for the body. As far as your coffee intake goes, you can keep it to about twice or thrice a week. That should be ok. But again, it's your body, so you decide.

A moderate intake of caffeine should not interfere with the benefits you get by practicing mindfulness meditation.

The effects of meditation and caffeine consumption are exactly the opposite. Caffeine stimulates your brain and triggers your fight or flight mode, and keeps you running as if somebody is out to get you. Excess consumption of caffeine can cause restlessness, stress, and even anxiety. Whereas in the case of meditation, the brain activity slows down, and as a result, you feel calm. You see, the very purpose of mindfulness and meditation is to keep your mind in a restful state. When you meditate, you first still your body, and that in turn stills your mind. You don't need an adrenaline rush to achieve that state. Be free of thoughts, worry, and anxiety.

If you consume too much caffeine, you are likely to have disturbed sleep at night (most people have that effect), and you're more likely to drift into sleep during your meditation sessions. A good night's sleep along with a well-relaxed body is important before you sit down for meditation. Many people claim that caffeine does not have any impact on their sleep. But how do we know?

How do you know that you sleep well at night? It's not about how you feel when you get up in the morning, but it's about how you feel for the rest of the day, what kind of thoughts you generate, how do you handle difficult situations, and what kind of decisions you make. If you cannot get started without caffeine, you are hooked for sure. You are the slave of your own habit, which you picked up. It defeats the whole purpose of setting oneself free from indulgences that cause pain.

It totally depends on your goal in life. If you are practicing meditation just for mental health benefits, a cup of coffee every other day is unlikely to have any major impact.

How To Balance the Creative Ideas in The Mind with the Indifference Needed in Meditation?

Nothing is needed in meditation. Meditation is not an activity to achieve an outcome. When we sit for meditation, we simply allow whatever arises in consciousness. Trying to hold on to an outcome, like an expectation of indifference, is not meditation.

We're not in meditation when we sit with our eyes closed. We're not in meditation when we see thoughts appearing in awareness. We're in meditation when the meditator disappears, and all that remains is the presence or the empty awareness. Although you didn't specify what you mean by indifference, I assume, from the context, that it is indifference towards the thinking mind. What you refer to as indifference, I call witnessing. There's a difference between observation and witnessing. When observing thoughts, there's an observer or sense of personal self that identifies with a particular set of thoughts and condemns the others. The observer continuously labels, judges, and sometimes even reacts to thoughts.

"I like this," "I don't like that," "I should not be thinking all this," "meditation is useless," "why am I wasting my time sitting here with eyes closed when I can be productive and write something." The observer clearly distinguishes between what's desirable and what's not. However, witnessing is impersonal. When witnessing happens, there's no individual analyzing the contents of the mind. The ego or the personal self drops the resistance, realizing that it's not the creator of thoughts. It watches ceaselessly without labeling, judging, or reacting to anything. Therefore, the indifference you're talking about is not a state that the mind can forcefully sustain. However, in your particular case, the creativity wants to unleash.

So why offer resistance? Watch it all. Let the mind exhaust. It's a sign that your creative center is awakening. The story ideas come to you because the creative energy tries to express itself. After meditation, write those ideas on paper and contemplate them. That's not the problematic thinking mind but the working mind in action. The meditation creates a space for these ideas to appear from the vast depths of the mind.

I have gone through this phase myself. Allow these ideas to emerge and channel them through a medium like books, podcasts, or whatever you prefer.

However, if there's an apprehension about how others will perceive the ideas, that's the thinking mind in action.

Again, it's not undesirable or desirable. It simply is "what is." Most people feel sleepy in meditation (which is expected in the early stages as the mind's conscious surface begins to calm), but your mind seems to be activated. And that's okay.

Let that creative energy flow. Don't worry about how the meditation is progressing. The idea of meditation is not to become a good meditator. If you become a good meditator and convince yourself that you're in peace, the ego will find a backdoor entry, which can be devasting. The peace (or indifference) will happen.

[1] https://mindfulnessquest.com/8-sattvic-superfoods-for-healthy-body-and-mind/

About The Author

Jagjot Singh is a mindfulness and meditation speaker and writer. He writes in-depth articles on his website https://mindfulnessquest.com.

He speaks and writes about one of the oldest eastern teachings known as *Advaita*, which nowadays is called Non-Duality. Additionally, he writes on topics such as chakra healing, mindfulness, spirituality, development, and more, in his blog and YouTube channel. If you have any questions or queries, please feel free to get in touch.

You can directly reach out to Jagjot via email: info@mindfulness.com

Printed by Libri Plureos GmbH in Hamburg, Germany